Lancashire and Cumbria by Rail

A guide to the routes, scenery and towns

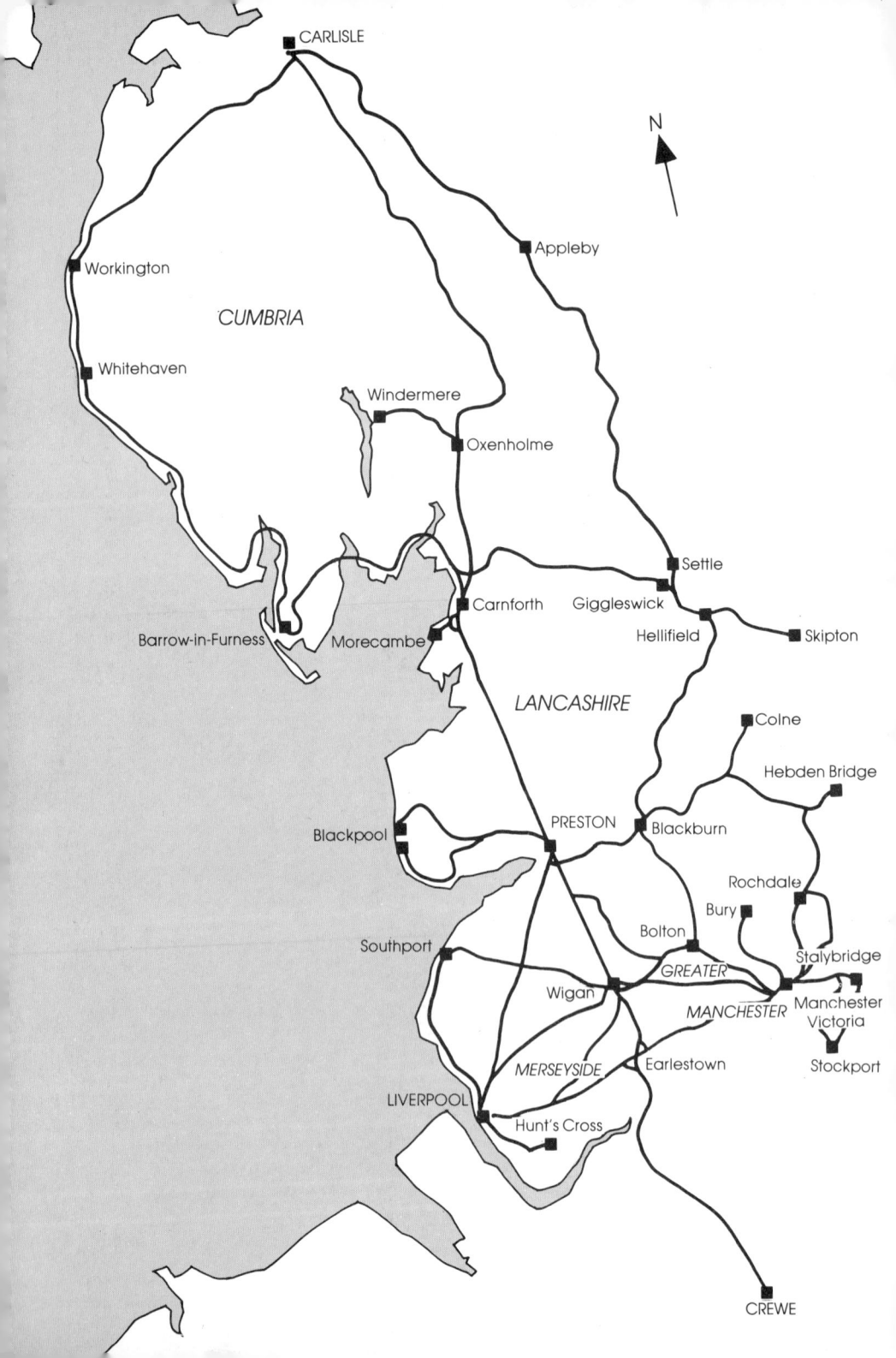

CONTENTS

Editor's introduction	4
Crewe–Preston by Tim Young	5
Preston–Carlisle by George Boyle	8
Wigan–Southport by Tim Young	11
Preston–Blackpool North by Malcolm Richardson	12
Kirkham and Wesham–Blackpool South by Paul Nettleton and Malcolm Richardson	14
Preston–Colne by Tim Young	17
Blackburn–Hellifield by Richard Watts	18
Lancaster–Morecambe by Tim Young	20
Carnforth–Skipton by Tim Young	21
Oxenholme–Windermere by Tim Young and Malcolm Conway	23
Carlisle–Carnforth via Barrow by Lloyd Daniels, Trevor Garrod and Richard Watts	24
Settle–Carlisle by Stan Abbott	29
Manchester Victoria–Liverpool Lime Street by Andrew Macfarlane	34
Earlestown–Warrington Bank Quay by Andrew Macfarlane	37
Southport–Liverpool Central by Tim Young	38
Liverpool Central–Preston via Ormskirk by Geoffrey Nelson	39
Wigan–Liverpool Central via Kirkby by Andrew Macfarlane	42
Liverpool Lime Street–Wigan via St Helens Central by Andrew Macfarlane	44
Liverpool Central–Hunts Cross via St Michaels by Andrew Macfarlane	45
Manchester Victoria–Wigan via Atherton by Andrew Macfarlane	46
Manchester Victoria–Preston via Chorley by Andrew Macfarlane and Malcolm Richardson	49
Bolton–Wigan by Andrew Macfarlane	51
Blackburn–Bolton by Tim Young	51
Manchester Victoria–Bury, including A Walk Round Heaton Park and Around Rochdale by Felix Schmid	52
Hebden Bridge–Rose Grove and Manchester Victoria by Tim Young	55
Rochdale–Manchester Victoria via Oldham by Felix Schmid	57
Stalybridge–Manchester Victoria by Felix Schmid	59
Stockport–Stalybridge by Felix Schmid	60
The Blackpool Tramway by Malcolm Richardson	62
The East Lancashire Railway by Felix Schmid	63
The Railways of the Isle of Man by Alan McGiffin	64
The Lakeside & Haverthwaite Railway by Tim Young	67
The Ravenglass & Eskdale Railway by Douglas Ferreira	68
The Yorkshire Dales Railway by John Keavey	70
The Fylde Coast–a brief guide by Tim Young	71
Lancaster, Morecambe, and Heysham by Tim Young	72
Liverpool by Andrew Macfarlane	73
Manchester by Andrew Macfarlane	74
Preston by Richard Watts	76
Southport by Tim Young	77
Further Information	77
Come and Join Us!	79
Index	80

EDITOR'S INTRODUCTION

Welcome to North West England, especially if it is your first visit to this beautiful part of the country. However, you may have visited the region before – a business trip to either Liverpool or Manchester, an excursion to see the world-famous Blackpool illuminations, or a peaceful holiday amid the green hills of the Lake District – this book will take you to all these and other places besides. Starting with a ride north from Crewe to the historic and interesting Border city of Carlisle, exploring branch lines to such places as Southport, Morecambe and Windermere, then riding along the route from Manchester to Liverpool made famous by George Stephenson's *Rocket* during the Rainhill Trials of 1830, before exploring the northern commuter routes into those two cities. There are brief sketches of important and interesting towns and cities, designed to whet your appetite sufficiently to visit them and find out more about them, and finally there are the private and preserved lines although the Blackpool Tramways are neither private nor preserved, being owned by the local authority and a normal means of public transport, with from time to time, new trams being added to the fleet. Maybe though, you have never been to the North West and even now are reading this book in some other part of the country. If that is the case, I hope that with this book we can tempt you to visit us and that, having come once, you will then return many more times.

I could not have edited this book without the help of many friends whom I shall now embarrass by mentioning by name. First and foremost, Trevor Garrod, whose experience, having published several railguides himself in the past for other areas of the country, made his advice invaluable; the Chairman of the NW branch of the RDS, Richard Watts, for his support; Andrew MacFarlane for his tireless enthusiasm and plethora of contributions; Tom Heavyside and John Sommerfield the main suppliers of photographs for the book; and the various rail users' associations in the region, especially Geoffrey Nelson and OPTA, Malcolm Richardson and SFLUA, Stan Abbott and FOSCLA, Malcolm Conway and LLAG, and Lloyd Daniels and the other members of the Derwent Railway Society. I should like to thank also the other contributors to this book, George Boyle and Felix Schmid and Steven Binks for the line diagrams, plus all the help and information provided by the Lakeside and Haverthwaite Railway Company, the Ravenglass & Eskdale Railway Company, and the Yorkshire Dales Railway Company. Thanks, too, to Alan McGiffin for his very interesting rail tour round the Isle of Man. Lastly, but by no means least, my thanks must go to my long-suffering wife for her tolerance over the past few months.

Finally, to those readers resident in the North West, I hope you feel we have done your local line and your town credit. I hope you, too, will find inspiration in the pages which follow, to explore different parts of the region and to leave your car at home or, at worst, in your local station's car park.

British Rail do sell a Runabout ticket each summer valid for seven days and covering all the lines featured in this book except Crewe to Warrington. In 1987 it will cost £24, and also entitles the holder to discounts on admission to several private steam lines and other tourist attractions.

Tim Young, Penwortham, January 1987

Front cover: A DMU crosses the Leven Viaduct (*Photo:* Tom Heavyside)
Back cover: Sunset over Windermere, Cumbria (*Photo:* T. Parker)
Inside front cover: Lancaster Castle (*Photo:* D. Avon)
Inside back cover: A streamliner tramcar passing Blackpool Tower during the illuminations (*Photo:* Malcolm Richardson)
Title page: Cunard Building, Liverpool (*Photo:* D. Avon)

CREWE–PRESTON
by Tim Young

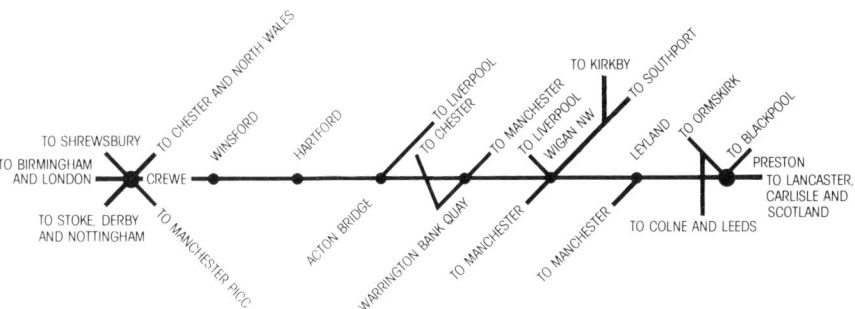

Crewe, the most well-known junction on the British Rail network, is the start of our journey through North West England. Once a sleepy little village deep in the heart of rural Cheshire, it quickly grew into a town with the arrival of the railways in the middle of the last century. Today, six routes converge on the town, three of them electrified. If you are travelling to the North West, be it on business or for pleasure, from the south, the probability is that you will have to go via Crewe. One route runs virtually due south to Birmingham and London, one goes south-west to Shrewsbury, one heads east to Stoke, Derby, Nottingham and Lincoln (in that order), one more to the west via Chester and the North Wales coast to its eventual terminus at Holyhead, the fifth going north-east to Manchester while the route we will be taking goes due north to Liverpool, Preston, Carlisle and into Scotland. Most trains to Preston do not start at Crewe but come up either from London or from places as far away as Penzance and Swansea via Birmingham. While we wait for our train to arrive, let us have a brief look round the station. For six weeks in June and July 1985, the station was completely shut down except for one or two shuttle services, and completely refitted. You will not fail to notice how bright and airy the various buffets, bookstalls, waiting-rooms, and toilets are. All the track, overhead catenary, and signalling was also removed, and relaid to modern specifications so that trains which do not stop at Crewe can run through the station at 80 m.p.h., considerably faster than they were able to before. Despite all that is new and modern, there are also signs of the station's history. In the shadow of the main station footbridge at the north end of the station, you will find a charming little drinking-trough for dogs on Platform 5.

However, it is time to head north. As we leave the station, sets of lines sweep off to both left and right. Those to the left go to Chester and Holyhead, and those to the right go to Manchester. Both those lines are described in detail in *Cheshire and North Wales By Rail*. In the 'fork' of the junction on your right is Crewe speedway track and in the left hand fork is the Crewe Heritage Centre due to be opened by H.M. the Queen in July 1987, while if you look back towards Crewe on your left at this stage you will see the tall office block of Rail House which is adjacent to the station and houses, among other things, the Regional Control Office, which oversees all train movements throughout the region. Also on your left you will start to notice overhead catenary right down at track-level apparently, though it soon climbs away to reveal running lines coming up from below to join up with ours. These are the avoiding lines which run round the back of Crewe Station to rejoin the main line at a large freight yard called Basford Hall to the south of Crewe. They formed a vital part of the arrangements for the closure of Crewe for those six weeks in 1985 when all trains from the north used them to bypass the station. Within a few minutes we are leaving the newer housing on the northern outskirts of the town and not long after speed through Winsford and subsequently Hartford, the former connected with salt-mining. Soon lines come in from our right which form a spur for freight trains to run direct to Northwich on the Manchester–Chester line which we will have just gone under. Next we pass the rustic little halt of Acton Bridge, looking somewhat out of place on one of the busiest main lines in the country. We cross the River Weaver, before passing Weaver Junction signal-box, the junction itself soon following. This is where the routes to Preston and Liverpool go their separate ways, and you will see a single line separate away to both right and left. You may just see the 'signpost' on the line going to your left saying 'To Liverpool', while the line going off to the right climbs up before turning left to cross over the top of our lines. Racing on through pleasant countryside our next point of interest is a high embankment to our left bringing lines in from that direction and over the top of ours. These come in from Chester and after crossing the West Coast main line run parallel with it (though out of sight) before joining up with it farther on at Acton Grange Junction. Very soon, though, lines go away to our right once more, this time to go to Walton Old freight yard which you will see down below on your right with the Laporte chemical works and Thames case factories in the background. You may notice a cluster of eight large cooling towers on the distant left-hand skyline, these are the Fiddlers Ferry power-station. Ever since Acton Grange Junction our train will have been braking and now comes the reason why as we run into Warrington Bank Quay Station. Soon after we leave Bank Quay Station we pass under the line from Manchester to Liverpool via Warrington's other station which has the suffix 'Central'. After going under the M62 motorway, we come to Winwick Junction where we bear to the right while lines bear away to the left. These are used by Manchester–Chester via Warrington trains as well as being a useful diversionary route for main-line trains. After running up to Earlestown, they turn right towards Manchester and then after Newton-le-Willows Station turn left at Parkside West Junction to rejoin our line at Golborne Junction. The importance of this diversionary route is shown by the fact that Earlestown to Parkside is the only portion of the main line from Liverpool to Manchester to be electrified apart from the first few miles out of Liverpool which are also used by London trains.

Soon we are going under the Manchester–Liverpool line and if you are very observant you may just catch a glimpse of the overhead catenary on it, but you will need to be quick as we are now running at speed again. Lines soon come in from the right to join ours and this is Golborne Junction, previously mentioned. We cross the Leeds–Liverpool Canal, pass Bamfurlong sidings on the left, then lines sweep in from Liverpool also on our left as we also pass Springs Branch depot on our right where there is often a good variety of locomotives to be seen. Lines coming in from the right seem to bounce off ours as they disappear again almost as soon as they join ours. We are pulling in to Wigan's North Western Station, the suffix a reminder of the companies that operated railways in this part of the world before the 1923 Grouping, while the lines that we briefly saw to our right descend into a tunnel before running into Wigan's other station, Wallgate. They come from Manchester and are described in detail later in this book as are the lines from Liverpool that we have just encountered, too.

Wigan is most famous for its pier, not a source of seaside entertainment for we are still some distance from the sea, but a place where goods could be loaded and unloaded from the various boats that used to ply up and down the canal in its heyday. Only pleasure-craft use the canal today though and the warehouses and other buildings round the pier have been transformed into a very interesting tourist attraction, so interesting in fact that in 1986 it was officially opened by Her Majesty the Queen and

An express train to Glasgow passes Springs Branch depot, Wigan, on 21 June 1984 (*Photo:* Tom Heavyside).

given a major award by the English Tourist Board. There are water buses, an exhibition entitled *The Way We Were*, the largest working steam-engine in the world at Trencherfield Mill, and many other attractions not least of which are the pleasantly landscaped canal-side walks. All this is within easy reach of either Wigan station. If you leave Wigan North Western Station, firstly note the Pelican crossing about 50 yards up the road to your right. The main entrance to Wallgate Station is on the other side of the road by this crossing. However, to get to the pier, you should stay on the North Western side of the road and walk down the hill to your left. You will come to the Wigan Pier complex at the bottom of the hill which is not too steep for your return to either station afterwards. As we leave Wigan for the final leg of our journey to Preston, Wallgate Station can be clearly seen in a cutting down on our right, while if you look to your left you will see the lines from Wallgate fork in two, the left-hand ones going to Kirkby of *Z-Cars* fame, and the right-hand ones going to Southport. Wigan Cricket Club's Ground is alongside the line to the right, while two sets of four floodlight pylons soar above the rooftops, one set on either side of the line. Those to our left are those of Springfield Park, home of Wigan Athletic Football Club, while those to our right are those of Central Park, home of Wigan Rugby League Club. Soon we are racing through the town of Coppull which used to have a station until 1969. Coppull is easily recognised by the large mill building on our left, no longer used as such, but a home for several small businesses, and a pub right alongside the line on our right called 'The Royal Scot'. After Coppull slow lines separate away to the left, running parallel to ours but a short distance away, as we pass the residential area of Balshaw Lane before we come to Euxton (the 'u' is silent) where lines come in from the right to join us having come up from Manchester. Then we are under the M6 and through Leyland with just a few miles to go. Leyland Trucks, part of the Rover Group are to our left before lines curve away to the right giving direct access to East Lancs

7

for freight trains and special excursions from the south. The pretty little church in the village of Farington can be seen to the left as the houses of Lostock Hall peep over a high embankment to our right. Lines come in from our left to join us at Farington Curve Junction having come from East Lancs, Leeds & Ormskirk. We are slowing down as we go under the aptly named Skew Bridge, before Preston spreads out before us on the skyline. Playing-fields lie below us to the right, with the relics of railways of yester-year beyond in the form of trackless embankments. On our left are the houses of Penwortham and then we are trundling across the girder bridge and into Preston Station. On the left can be seen Preston's main sorting office which has direct access to the station facilitating the transport of mail by rail, while on our right just before the station there is a pleasant area of parkland alongside the River Ribble which we crossed while on the girder bridge. At the time of writing, Preston Station is in a state of flux, with repair and renovation work in progress. If you go up the dozen or so stairs to your right after going through the ticket barrier, you will leave the station and have the Fishergate shopping centre in front of you, housing Asda and Debenhams to name just two of the stores in this brand-new complex.

PRESTON – CARLISLE
by George Boyle

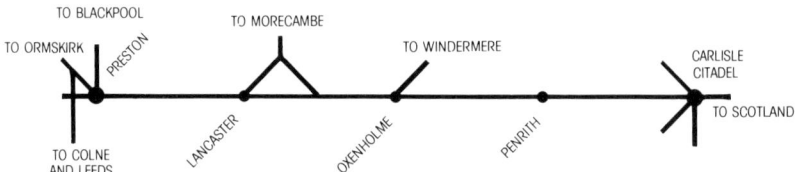

Our journey starts at Preston which was once a thriving cotton town. Now the cotton has mostly gone to be replaced by a variety of light industries. The largest employers in the town now are British Aerospace and GEC Traction who, more likely than not, manufactured the electrical equipment for the locomotive at the head of our train. It is about to whisk us to Carlisle in a little over one hour, non stop, for a journey of some 90 miles. Compared to the High Speed Trains of the Western and Eastern Regions this may not appear spectacular, but as the journey unfolds we will see how sinuous the route is. Joseph Locke, who engineered the line, did a marvellous job in constructing it without a tunnel but in the era of HSTs we are beginning to pay the price in speed restrictions on the many curves of the route.

As we glide quietly out of the station under Fishergate Bridge look out of the left-side window towards the locomotive. Quickly, before the train rounds the curve and obscures the view we will see St Walburge's Church steeple, at 315 feet the third highest in England. On a clear day its white limestone faces shine out and can be seen for miles. On a winter's night, when conditions are correct, the northern lights can be seen dancing on its white surfaces. It was designed by Hansom of Hansom cab fame, and it stands on a foundation of the original stone sleepers from the first track laid on the Preston – Lancaster line and later replaced by timber. Just before we pass the church, the line to Blackpool curves away to our left and we disappear through a tiny arch bridge which defies the status of the 'Premier Line' to Carlisle. Gathering speed we have an open view to our left and beyond the viaduct of the Blackpool line in the distance once stood the cranes of the now-closed Preston Dock, in its day the largest single dock in the country. Soon we will be accelerating to the maximum speed on this line of 110 mph.

As the countryside opens out around us, to our left we have the fertile plain of the Fylde and occasional glimpses, on a good day, of Blackpool Tower in the far distance. To our right we have rolling Fells rising to just short of 2,000 feet which give the lie to the stories that Lancashire is all cotton-mills and coal-mines. Several times on our journey we will pass over the Preston–Kendal Canal, once a thriving waterway but robbed of its goods traffic by the emerging railways it is now a haven for pleasure cruising and anglers.

About 7 miles north of Preston we come alongside the M6 motorway. We will see it again several times on our journey to Carlisle. As we speed along in safety 40 mph faster than the legal maximum on the adjacent motorway we can only wonder at the folly that allows the railway, so recently electrified and modernised, to be so under-utilised while the constant stream of lorries and coaches trundles slowly alongside us.

In less than twenty minutes we are approaching Lancaster. On the right-hand side set in its own parkland on a hill is the green copper dome of the Ashton Memorial, built by the unemployed in the cotton famine as a gift by Lord Ashton, a major city benefactor. As we draw into Lancaster it is noticeable that stone has replaced brick as the primary building material and it becomes apparent that this city has suffered the ravages of the Industrial Revolution far less than other Lancashire towns farther south. We can change trains at Lancaster to visit the nearby seaside resort of Morecambe and the port of Heysham for the boat to the Isle of Man. Lancaster is also where we have to change for Barrow-in-Furness and Skipton because, as we shall shortly see, Carnforth, to the north, is now only served by local trains from Lancaster. While we are standing in Lancaster Station we can see to the right Lancaster Castle towering above us. Today it is used as a Crown Court and prison. Assizes have been held here since 1176 and more people have probably been sentenced to death here than anywhere else in England, including ten Lancashire witches and 240 people in the four years after the Battle of Waterloo. Just as we pull out of the station, on the right is the heavily overgrown branch line to Green Ayre and Morecambe by a now-closed route. This line was the test-bed for the 25,000 volt overhead line electrification which we have to thank for the modern system of travelling we are travelling under today.

Immediately on leaving Lancaster we pass over the River Lune. Here it is a large tidal river and to our left is a small quay which occasionally sees a small coaster. The next time we see the Lune it will be a very different river. Accelerating again to maximum speed the line to Morecambe leaves from our left and soon we pass over the level crossing at Hest Bank. On our left is Morecambe Bay and across the water can be seen the hammer-head cranes of Barrow shipyard. Here we are at sea-level. Before Carlisle we will have ascended all but 1,000 feet and returned to sea-level again.

In less than 5 miles we will pass through Carnforth. Look to the left and you will see the old motive power depot, now Steamtown, and if you are lucky you will see one or more of the giants of steam moving in the yard. Carnforth is the junction for Barrow and Skipton but as we speed through the station we can see that the main-line platforms have been removed forcing passengers to change trains back at Lancaster. A feature of the line onwards to Carlisle is the absence of stations. We still have over 60 miles to travel but we will only pass through two intermediate stations. The local population must have objected to railway modernisation, with its consequent station closures, as much as they objected to the coming of the M6 motorway. Now the train is rising on a slight gradient and soon after passing through a hideous modern concrete road overbridge we leave Lancashire and enter Cumbria. Suddenly drystone walls are much in evidence and barns and farm buildings are built from a similar rubble stone.

Soon we are approaching Oxenholme, the junction for Windermere and the Lake District but we must visit there another day for the locomotive is now pulling hard as the climb to the hills has now begun in earnest. We are climbing now towards Grayrigg summit, the first of the two major hills to be conquered before Carlisle. In steam days we would have needed a banking engine but the electric locomotive makes light work of the climb. To our left we see Kendal in the valley bottom and in the distance the Lake District fells rising to over 3,000 feet.

Once over the summit at Grayrigg we pass under the M6 motorway as it joins us to our left for several miles to follow the only practicable route through these hills, discovered by Locke 125 years before the coming of the motorways. Now the road traffic is travelling as fast as we are. The sinuous route referred to earlier is forcing us to slow to their more pedestrian pace. Ninety-seven per cent of the line from Oxenholme to Penrith is curved track. Looking to our right we can see Low Gill Viaduct. Now out of use it once carried a branch to join the 'Little North Western' Midland Railway branch at Ingleton. Had the private railways co-operated more in earlier days this branch would have meant that the magnificent Settle–Carlisle line would never have been built. Now we are in the Lune Gorge. Low down to the right is a different Lune from that seen at Lancaster. This is wild water and good salmon-fishing too! The hills are closing in and soon we will have to climb again, but keep your eyes open to the right and on the far hillside you will see a peculiar heart-shaped wood known to railwaymen as 'The Heart of Westmorland'.

Passing through the village of Tebay we bridge the Lune, pass under the M6, and climb towards Shap summit. Here the ground is flat and windswept and soon after electrification was completed, extra masts had to be installed to stop the overhead wires losing contact with the locomotive pantograph in the strong winds. Approaching Shap summit we enter a rock cutting and high above us crosses a lattice girder bridge. To generations of footplatemen this was known as 'The Bridge of Sighs' for, having fired a steam locomotive from sea-level near Carnforth, they knew the hard work was over. At Shap summit (916 feet above sea-level) stand the Shap granite works and we immediately begin the fall back to sea-level at Carlisle. On our right we pass Hardendale Quarry which supplies trainloads of limestone for the steelworks at Ravenscraig, Motherwell. We pass through Shap village, again without a station, and through a succession of curves towards Penrith. The buildings are still made of stone but now are a beautiful dark red sandstone quarried locally. Just before Penrith we pass over the M6 twice in a short distance as the line curves through 90 degrees to enter the station. Once in Penrith we could have changed trains for Keswick and Workington but alas this line fell to the 'Beeching axe' and now the best we can hope for is a bus to Lake Ullswater. Immediately ouside the station are the ruins of a fourteenth-century castle. On Beacon Hill, to the right, stands the watch-tower, built in 1719. William Wordsworth went to school here and his mother is buried in the churchyard which contains a group of Saxon stones dating back 1,000 years.

On leaving Penrith we are on the last leg of our journey. Only 5 miles away to our right is the Settle–Carlisle line which will join us at Carlisle. Again to our right are the hills of the Pennine chain having their last fling before petering out at the Scottish border to be replaced by the Cheviots. On our left the Lake District fells have been replaced by more gentle hills. This country was conquered by the Romans and on one side of the line the A6 and on the other an unclassified road runs in the typically Roman straight line all the way to Carlisle. Approaching the city we pass over the M6 for the last time before slowing down. Soon we are entering the city and we can tell that this was a major railway centre. Before the Grouping seven railway companies converged here and together they built the main station, Carlisle Citadel. Carlisle is a worthy place to end our journey for it is steeped in history. Hadrian built his wall on the north bank of the River Eden and the city grew up round the Roman camp on the opposite bank. As we leave the station we are immediately confronted by the twin towers of the Citadel—very impressive but actually built in the nineteenth century as offices and courts. You must visit the cathedral with its magnificent choir and east window, one of the finest in England. Also worthy of a visit is the castle, still the home of an Army regiment. Richard III was the Governor here once and among the prisoners held here was Mary Queen of Scots. Tullie House Museum and St Cuthbert's Church are also worth seeing, but we will need more than one day to take in all the delights of the Border City.

Going farther afield, we could catch a train bound for Newcastle and alight at Haltwhistle or Hexham to catch a bus to Hadrian's Wall. This fortification was built by the Romans and originally stretched from Bowness on the Solway Firth to Wallsend on Tyneside.

WIGAN–SOUTHPORT
by Tim Young

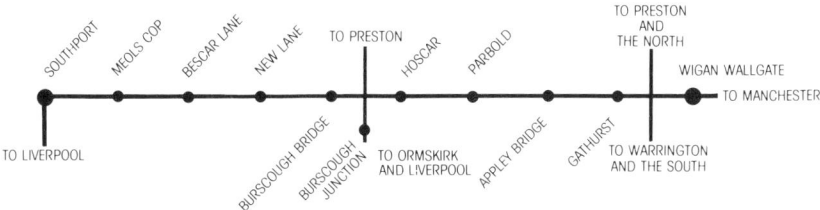

Wigan, an industrial town, situated on the Leeds–Liverpool Canal and roughly equidistant from the two major cities of Liverpool and Manchester has an unenviable and totally undeserved reputation, so much so that in the summer of 1986, Wigan's publicity department produced a brochure entitled *I've never been to Wigan but I know what it's like*. Its most well-known attraction is its pier, which won the British Tourist Authority 'Come to Britain' Award a few months after being opened officially as a tourist attraction by Her Majesty the Queen in the spring of 1986. It is well worth a visit, with canal-side walks, museums, water buses, and several other attractions. It is but a short walk from either of the two Wigan rail stations. If you're arriving at the North Western Station, come out of the station and turn left down the hill, and if you are arriving at Wallgate, turn right as you come out of the station and go down the hill, and the pier complex is at the bottom of the hill—(which is not too steep)—and about ten minutes' walk away. The two stations mentioned are in fact about 50 yards apart on opposite sides of the same main road, so the safest way to cross Wigan is by means of the Pelican crossing outside Wallgate Station to which we will now return for the journey to the coast.

The train will have commenced its journey at Manchester Victoria Station, travelling via Atherton or Westhoughton, both lines having been covered in detail elsewhere. As we leave we immediately pass underneath the West Coast main line which overshadows Wallgate at its west end. Almost immediately the lines fork in two with lines to Kirkby disappearing to our left, while we curve to the right. We come to the first station at Gathurst while still on the outskirts of Wigan, before crossing the Leeds–Liverpool Canal and going under the M6 simultaneously. The canal then runs alongside the line on the left for most of the way to the next halt at Appley Bridge.

One can alight here for a very pleasant walk through the lovely wooded Douglas Valley to Parbold and then through open country to Burscough, following the Leeds–Liverpool Canal all the way. The canal is still with us as we leave Appley Bridge although we lose it as we approach Parbold. After Parbold, we pass through pleasant agricultural country, calling at the village station of Hoscar then, farther on, we cross the canal once more before passing underneath the Preston–Ormskirk line. Almost at once we are at Burscough Bridge Station. Martin Mere Wildfowl Trust is a few miles away now, and a bus goes there from Burscough. After leaving Burscough, the scene once more becomes sparsely populated with just two wayside halts at New Lane and Bescar Lane before the outskirts of Southport are reached and we pull in to the island platform of Meols Cop. We are nearly at journey's end now but before we get to Southport, we pass the sheds of the former Southport Derby Road depot on our right which are now the premises of Steamport Southport. If you are at all interested in railways and railway restoration then this is certainly worth a visit. Special events are arranged throughout the summer and you should inquire locally for further details. But now we are pulling into Southport, with the electric train waiting on our left if we intend travelling down the coast to Liverpool.

PRESTON–BLACKPOOL NORTH
by Malcolm Richardson

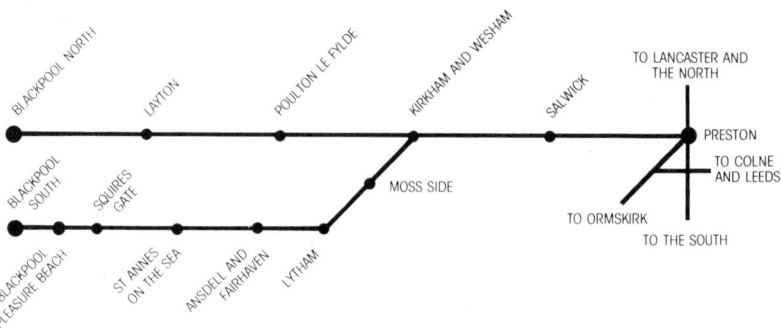

Leaving Preston, we pass County Hall on the left, then Preston power signal box that controls all movements of trains west to Salwick, north to Tebay and south towards Warrington. Taking the Blackpool line to the left, while the West Coast main line trails off to the right at Fylde Junction, we pass the impressive spire of St Walburge's Church on the right, then soon passing over Maudland Viaduct we are offered a good view of Preston Docks. Clearly visible is *The Manxman*, a former Isle of Man ferry which used to ply between Fleetwood and Douglas, now permanently moored here. It has been transformed into an exclusive night-club and high-class restaurant since its retirement. Also on the left can be seen the English Electric works, and on the right we run parallel with the new Ingol Bypass.

Gathering speed we soon reach the rapidly expanding new housing estate of Lea. This suburb of Preston had its own station until 1938 and there is much speculation about the value of reopening it. Passing through pleasant Fylde farmlands we approach, on the left, British Nuclear Fuel's Springfield works. Most trains will pass through the next station at Salwick which once had an attractive island platform with buildings, and positioned at the far end, a unique wishing-well surrounded by flower-

Poulton le Fylde Station (*Photo:* Malcolm Richardson)

beds. All the buildings were removed in the late 1970s, though the canopies, strangely, still survive.

Soon we arrive at Kirkham. Continuing to Kirkham North Junction, the branch line to Blackpool South via the coast trails away to the left. Once past the signal-box, the train passes the site of the former 'flying junction' that carried the direct line from Blackpool South via Bradkirk from a deep cutting. It is now used as a ballast tip and few would realise its former use. Taking the sweeping curve to the right, we pass under the M55 motorway bridge to Blackpool. By the next overbridge can be seen Weeton signal-box. Having passed yet another overbridge that carries the road to Weeton, the train is now on a long straight stretch of track, heading towards Singleton. On the left, Blackpool Tower can be seen in the distance, and on the right we pass Singleton signal-box. There was also a station here at one time but all signs have now been totally removed. After a short time, the train starts to slow for Poulton which still boasts a long island platform. The main station buildings and canopy are the last surviving example of a typical island platform station in the area and the large clock is to be restored with financial assistance from Lancashire County Council. Poulton is an ancient market town; in the square can be found stocks, a whipping-post and a Market Cross. It is a favourite retirement area and still holds a considerable population commuting to Preston and Manchester. Beyond the station the line divides and to the right at Poulton signal-box it trails off to the sadly truncated remains of the former main line to Fleetwood, named after Peter Hesketh Fleetwood. Opened in 1840, it helped to transform a 'rabbit warren' into a major fishing port and was the northern terminus of West Coast train services. The North Euston Hotel in Fleetwood was where passengers stayed the night before completing the journey to Glasgow by sea. All train services to Fleetwood ceased in 1966. Now only infrequent freight trains operate to Thornton ICI works.

Heading towards Blackpool from Poulton we pass Carleton crossing with its neat little signal-box, then approach Layton Station, formerly called 'Bispham', which once counted the late Violet Carson, Ena Sharples of *Coronation Street*, as its most famous regular commuter to Manchester. Taking a slight incline, we reach Devonshire Road bridge, and Blackpool North No.1 signal-box on the left. On the right can be seen Enfield Road carriage sidings, once completely full of coaching stock and visiting excursion traffic. Today, due to intensive train diagrams, there are seldom more than two rakes of carriages to be seen. Passing Blackpool North No.2 signal-box on the right, the train enters the 'throat' of Blackpool North Station. It was reconstructed in 1974 utilising the old 1938 LMS excursion platforms. The new station consists of eight platforms and a main passenger reception hall. After having passed through the ticket barrier it is rather like entering a vast greenhouse. New passenger information visual display units were installed in 1986 and the information office updated. On leaving the station, you will notice the Fine Fare supermarket that was built on the site of the former station. It was renamed from Talbot Road to Blackpool North in 1932 and demolished in 1974. Walking down Talbot Road, the bus station is on the left, where buses to various parts of the Fylde can be caught. Talbot Road contains more pubs than almost any other road in Blackpool, so there are no excuses for feeling thirsty around here! Talbot Road brings us to the North Pier, the trams, and all Blackpool's attractions.

KIRKHAM AND WESHAM – BLACKPOOL SOUTH
by Paul Nettleton and Malcolm Richardson

Kirkham and Wesham is a typical island station. The buildings have, however, in 1986, been extensively cleaned, with financial assistance from Lancashire County Council, bringing up the original colour of the yellow and red brick to good effect. The train from Blackpool South will usually be formed of a Class 142 Pacer unit, operating a basic hourly service.

On leaving Kirkham, to the left is the Railway Hotel, a well-known local watering-hole. On the right is Fox's biscuit works – renowned for their quality. Farther to the left is all that remains of Kirkham's once-extensive goods yard and sidings. Just ahead, Kirkham North Junction – the traditional railway gateway to the Fylde coast, where final routing of trains to Blackpool South via the coast line takes place – has a signal-box, once the most important in the Fylde area, that controls train movements here.

Taking the old up line, we enter the now entirely single-track branch line to Blackpool South. All the down-line section to beyond Moss Side was finally lifted in June 1986. Passing underneath the overbridge of the A583 Preston – Blackpool road, itself eclipsed by the M55 opened in 1975, we reach the next overbridge which marks the site of the once-pleasant village station of Wrea Green. Closed in 1961, it is currently the subject of a proposed reopening scheme. All traces of the old station have been swept away. Wrea Green which has expanded a great deal in both population and property since 1961, has won Lancashire's Best-kept Village award, and still boasts a very popular hostelry famed for its Boddington beers, The Grapes.

The village is only a mile's brisk walk from the next station, Moss Side, reopened in November 1983, and replacing the original station, closed in 1961. The station reopening scheme was carried out with financial assistance from Lancashire County Council, and has proved useful to visitors to the nearby hospital.

Shortly after Moss Side, a first distant glimpse of the famous Blackpool Tower is

Lytham Windmill (*Photo:* Malcolm Richardson)

afforded. After travelling on a section of embankment, the track is slewed across on to the old down-line alignment before we arrive at 'leafy' Lytham. A very opulent station used to adorn the area here in keeping with rows of ultra-respectable Victorian villas in a sylvan setting. The station has a classic frontage with awnings over both platforms. The staff were often complimented for the station's cleanliness and fine displays of flower-beds and hanging baskets. It became just another of BR's infamous unmanned halts in March 1971, and has in the intervening period declined into something approaching a ruin. Fortunately work to transform the building into a high-class pub has been completed. The impressive, though neglected, facade will be retained and has been refurbished in a most sympathetic manner on completion. The pleasant main street of Lytham is a bustling shopping centre and is just a stone's throw from the station. Half a mile away is Lytham Windmill, built in 1805 and recently restored, it sits at the centre of Lytham Green and overlooks the Ribble Estuary. It is open to the public during the season. Other attractions include Lowther Gardens and Pavilion which provide well-laid-out gardens along with indoor shows and exhibitions throughout the year.

As we depart, we see a new car park on the left. This area was once a bay platform where the Lytham motor train departed. This strange little locomotive with a single coach provided a shuttle to Blackpool Central. Introduced in 1913, it ran until the Second World War and was never reinstated. Continuing through the delightful Lytham Witch Wood, and under Skew Bridge, we approach the site of Ansdell goods yard, now covered by flats and an ambulance station. The next overbridge brings Ansdell and Fairhaven Station. Once an island platform with substantial buildings, it was sadly de-staffed in March 1971, and all the buildings demolished in 1972. With help from Lancashire County Council the platform has been resurfaced and a new waiting shelter provided. Walking from the station turn right at the top of the staircase and head direct to the promenade. Next to the station is Royal Lytham and St Annes

A Class 142 Pacer unit at the newly rebuilt St Annes-on-the-Sea Station on 30 September 1986 (*Photo:* Malcolm Richardson)

golf-course, famous for many tournaments.

The next station, St Annes, is the best appointed on the line, which once boasted fine facilities. In 1985, the station was completely demolished to make way for a Safeways supermarket, and a pleasing little replacement building has been erected. St Annes Square is an attractive shopping centre with many exclusive shops, a pier, and an open-air swimming pool.

Leaving St Annes, on the left stand the vandalised remains of the last signal-box, used on the line until 1983. Gathering speed, we pass St Annes Old Links golf-course. Close to this location was once a station called 'Gilletts Crossing Halt', closed in 1949. The next station, Squire's Gate, is used today by large numbers of visitors to the nearby Pontin's Holiday Camp, and is adjacent to Blackpool Airport, a point sadly neglected by the local council and British Rail.

Continuing through residential properties on both sides of the track, we approach Burlington Road Halt, closed in 1949 and reopened in April 1987 as the new Blackpool Pleasure Breach Station. There is suspicion this may be used as an excuse to close the line beyond here to Blackpool South. Approaching the last overbridge, we pass the site of the original South Shore Station. After alighting at Blackpool South, turn right at the top and by the second set of traffic lights you will find the Waterloo Hotel, famed for its bowling green. To the left, is the shopping centre, South Pier, Pleasure Beach, and, Blackpool's latest attraction, the Sandcastle Leisure Centre.

16

PRESTON–COLNE
by Tim Young

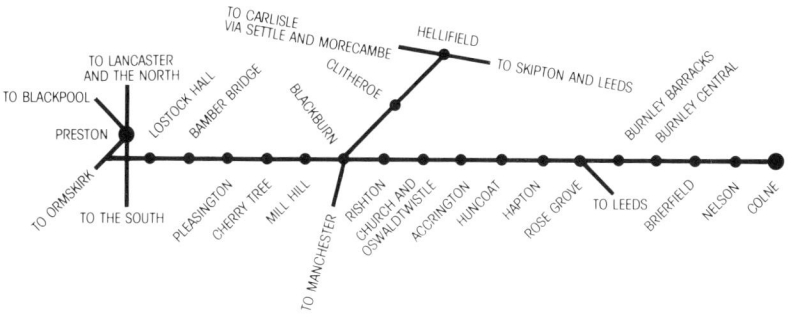

Our train stands in Platform 2 at Preston Station. Most trains to Colne leave from either Platforms 1 or 2 though other platforms can be used on occasion. The train is one of the new Pacer units recently introduced on North West local services. As we pull out of the station heading south, we pass the North Union sidings and the GPO sorting office on our right before crossing the River Ribble. Accelerating past the houses of Penwortham on our right, we soon pass under Skew Bridge before branching right at Farington Curve Junction where the lines divide almost immediately once more – so as we take to the left-hand lines, a single line goes off to the right, to Ormskirk and Liverpool. Meanwhile we are curving sharply to the left, passing Farington Church on our right before crossing over the West Coast main line.

The old Lostock Hall depot comes up on the right, then we are arriving at the first of many stops, Lostock Hall. Reopened in May 1984 on the opposite side of the bridge to a previous Lostock Hall Station, closed some years before, its basic facilities are nevertheless attractive, especially the red pantile roofing on the shelters. After Lostock Hall, new housing becomes very much apparent, instrumental in the reopening of the station. A line curves in from the right giving access to the line for trains to and from the south without the need to go to Preston and reverse.

The main Preston–Leyland road crosses the line and then, after passing Bamber Bridge sidings, the train arrives at Bamber Bridge Station. About a mile away is Cuerden Valley Country Park. On leaving Bamber Bridge, the train passes over a level crossing overshadowed by Bamber Bridge signal-box. This box also looks after three other crossings we will come to before the next station at Pleasington. The crossings will be Hospital crossing with the Hospital Inn near by on the left, Mintholme, and Hoghton, which is near Hoghton Tower. Unfortunately you will need to get a bus from Preston instead of a train to visit this fine example of a fortified house. The next station we come to though is Pleasington, and then Cherry Tree follows soon after. Mill Hill, the next station is on the outskirts of Blackburn, and is the nearest station to Ewood Park, home of Blackburn Rovers Football Club and as such is frequently the destination for soccer specials from all over the country. The cathedral town of Blackburn speads out before us as the 'West Pennine' line from Bolton via Darwen comes in on our right to meet us as we enter Blackburn Station. Only a few minutes' walk away is Blackburn Cathedral which among other items houses a rare medieval pax. There are several museums to visit, not to mention the shopping centre.

Leaving Blackburn, the train enters a tunnel, and soon after emerging into daylight

17

again, we come to a junction where lines curve off to the left. This is Daisyfield Junction, the lines to our left go to Clitheroe and Hellifield and, if you look carefully, you will get a brief glimpse of Daisyfield signal-box, several hundred yards up the branch. On our right, as we head on can be see several large DIY superstores. They originally wanted to be in Blackburn but the local authority were not willing to let them open on Sundays so they decided to base themselves in nearby Hyndburn. Just before Rishton Station we pass the local reservoir and then, after the next station that serves two small East Lancashire towns, Church and Oswaldtwistle, we approach Accrington at rooftop-level. The station is on a tight bend, so if you are getting on or off the train here, please watch the gap between the train and the platform. We snake across a twisting viaduct high above the town centre, the train's wheels squealing on the tight bends. On our left the scenery becomes more industrial with several factories.

We enter Huncoat Station going through a level crossing at the Preston end first. Backs of terraced houses overlook us to the right then we pass between a coal-mine on our left and a power-station on our right, both of which are now shut. Padiham power-station, however, is open and can be seen to the left. The M65 now runs alongside and at the next station, Hapton, a concrete footbridge crosses both the railway and the motorway to give access to houses otherwise separated from the station. There is a nice additional station nameplate made of small stones here. The town of Padiham can be seen clearly on the left skyline and soon a rusty single line joins us from the left, giving rail access to Padiham power-station. Sadly the rust bears all-too-evident testimony to the paucity of trains now serving it. The big island platform of Rose Grove Station comes next, with weed-ridden flower-beds at the Colne end. After Rose Grove the train rattles over Gannow Junction, taking the left-hand line while those lines to the right are the recently reopened Roses Link to Leeds. We soon come to Burnley Barracks Station and as Burnley lies below we enter Burnley Central. The Weavers Triangle and Toll House Museum will give you an insight into the history of the area, and how the Industrial Revolution brought prosperity to this corner of England. Even today there are many signs of Victorian engineering and industry though sadly most are left to the mercy of the elements and vandals. We are nearly at journey's end now, and after Brierfield, the next station, we come to Nelson. This town was named after Lord Horatio of Trafalgar Square fame. The town has a good shopping centre and the narrow cobbled streets with stone-built houses whose front doors open directly onto them will probably seem familiar. This is because the recent TV series *Juliet Bravo* was filmed in Nelson and other locations in the area. The train used to pause after leaving Nelson at Chaffers signal-box, to collect the branch staff as authority to proceed the final two miles along a single line to Colne. However in December 1986 the line was singled right through to Gannow Junction and the branch staff is not used any more. Colne is now the terminus of the line though before Beeching trains proceeded on to Skipton. However, the line has long since been closed and lifted. In Colne there is a British in India Museum, or you may decide to go on to Skipton by bus. For those interested in industrial history, the line is very interesting and even when in open country, the views can be quite superb.

BLACKBURN—HELLIFIELD
by Richard Watts

This must be the most difficult line to travel along. Currently, 1987, the only advertised passenger trains to use the line are the DalesRail services and between Preston and

Carlisle, which operate on seven Saturdays and three Sundays in the year. It is hard to imagine that in 1936 there was a half-hourly Blackburn–Clitheroe service with an almost hourly service onwards to Hellifield. In 1962 the line was closed to all regular passenger services and today the line is proposed for closure as part of the Settle–Carlisle line closure proposal.

Since 1962 attempts have been made to restore regular passenger services to this line. The latest efforts are currently being made by the Ribble Valley Rail Group set up by the Settle Carlisle Joint Action Committee. Various reports indicate that a restored passenger service to the Ribble Valley would be a viable proposition.

Despite the difficulties, a journey along this line is more than worthwhile. Planning beforehand, however, is essential – so obtain your DalesRail leaflet, book early, and arrive promptly to ensure getting a seat!

We will join the train at Blackburn Station. Very soon after leaving the cavernous Blackburn station the train goes into a tunnel and then the line turns sharply left. This is Daisyfield Junction, where the remains of the station, closed in 1958, can still be seen. The line takes us through Blackburn and on to the suburb of Wilpshire. After passing through Wilpshire Station (which is in excellent condition) and Tunnel we pass into the wide Ribble Valley. The River Ribble remains with us for the rest of the journey to Hellifield.

From Wilpshire onwards the scenery improves by the minute. We now pass Langho Station before crossing over the main road to Whalley and Clitheroe. Magnificent views can be had from the left of the train right across the Ribble Valley to Longridge Fell and Parlick (1,416 feet), which is part of the Forest of Bowland, distinguished by its pyramidal shape.

Shortly after Langho the train crosses the spectacular Whalley Viaduct. This has forty-eight arches, is 655 yards long, and is built of brick. The viaduct takes the line over the River Calder and there are fine views up and down the river. Before leaving the viaduct you will see the remains of Whalley Abbey on your right beside the north bank of the river. The viaduct was given Gothic details where the road to the Abbey gatehouse passes under it.

Whalley Abbey was founded in 1296 and has had a varied history. In 1537 it was converted into a Tudor manor house and today part is in ruins and the rest forms a conference centre and retreat house for the Blackburn Diocese. The town of Whalley is very compact and attractive.

From Whalley the line keeps to the right of the Ribble and takes us to the interesting market and administrative town of Clitheroe. The station was closed in 1962 but reopened for DalesRail in 1978. Clitheroe is a good base from which to explore Pendle Hill which dominates this area. Clitheroe Castle, visible from the train, was built in about 1180 by Robert de Lacy, Lord of Honor, and is one of the oldest stone structures in Lancashire. The castle commands good views and is now set in extensive grounds which contain a children's playground, tennis courts, a bowling-green, and the Castle Museum. About a mile from the station is the Edisford Recreation Area. Splendid walks by the Ribble can be had here.

North from Clitheroe the scenery is dominated by the Forest of Bowland, an Area of Outstanding Natural Beauty, on the left and Pendle Hill on the right. The line remains to the right of the River Ribble.

Soon after leaving Clitheroe you will see a siding on the left. This leads to the Clitheroe cement works and there are daily trains from here to Scotland. The factory chimneys are a dominant feature on the landscape and can be seen for miles.

Soon after leaving the cement works the train passes through the village of Chatburn. From Chatburn the line passes near to Rimington and then reaches the small town of Gisburn. North of the old station is the 156-yard-long Gisburn Tunnel, built to preserve Gisburn Park. The portals of the tunnel are worthy of note. Very soon the line passes through Newsholme and now approaches the Leeds–Settle–Carlisle line at Hellifield. This route is described in detail in another part of this book.

LANCASTER–MORECAMBE
by Tim Young

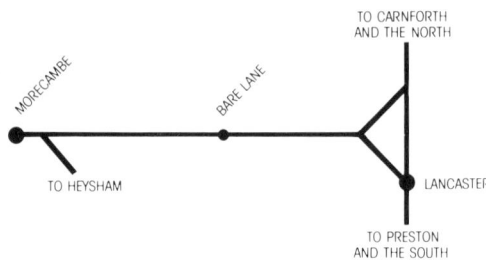

Our train stands in Platform 2 at Lancaster Station, a bay platform at the north end. To our left can be seen Lancaster City's Football Ground. The train moves off and swings on to the main line. We cross the River Lune and after 1¾ miles, as evidenced by the yellow mileposts alongside the line, we pass the colourlight signal giving access to the Morecambe branch. If you are sitting in the front seat of the train you may notice the diagonal line of five small white lights on top of the signal known as 'feathers' which, when illuminated, indicate that the points at the next junction are set to take the train off the main line in the direction in which the 'feathers' are pointing, in this case to the left. As we turn sharply to the left, our wheels squealing as we do so, another set of lines curve in from our right, giving trains from the north direct access to Morecambe without reversing. Until May 1984, most Morecambe–Leeds trains in either direction used this curve, but since that date they have all reversed at Lancaster.

The only passenger train to regularly use the north curve these days is the first train of the day from Carnforth to Lancaster which goes to Morecambe *en route* and then goes on to York via Manchester. Almost immediately after the lines converge from north and south, the train is pulling into the only intermediate station on the branch, Bare Lane. This little halt basically serves the residential areas of Bare and Torrisholme. At its west end, a signal box on the down platform oversees a level crossing. The train then continues on to Morecambe, passing through mainly residential areas. Shortly before it arrives at Morecambe, lines sweep in from the left which form the Heysham branch. In 1976 Sealink ceased sailing from Heysham to Belfast and at the same time British Rail also ceased passenger services to Heysham. In recent years, however, the tide has turned for the port of Heysham, with increased passenger sailings, especially to the Isle of Man. Because of this, representations were made to restore passenger services, and they resumed in May 1987. Morecambe telephone exchange can be seen on the right and the large and impressive Promenade signal-box on the left as we approach Morecambe Station. Amusement parks can be seen to both right and left, while straight ahead the impressive Midland Hotel dominates the skyline. The station itself, attractively stone built, is situated right on the sea front, ideally placed for those seeking the more traditional seaside amenities.

CARNFORTH – SKIPTON
by Tim Young

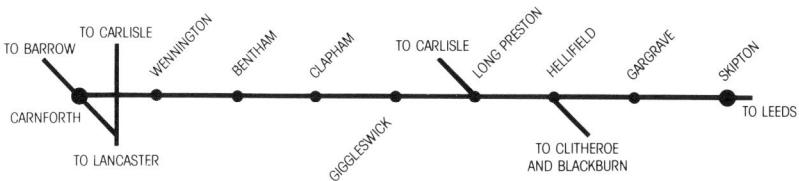

Most trains from Carnforth to Skipton will have started their journey at Morecambe and are continuing forward to Leeds. The line between Carnforth and Skipton passes through sparsely populated countryside. There are many features of particular note, the scenery being a mixture of peaceful pastureland, small villages whose houses are built of local stone, scattered areas of woodland and a succession of small yet fast-flowing rivers.

The train leaves Carnforth as if to go towards Barrow yet as soon as the platform end is cleared curves away to the right while the Barrow lines go away to the left. A signal-box stands in the 'V' created by this junction while a second box stands alongside the junction of the line the train is on and a line enabling trains to run direct between the Barrow line and the Skipton line without reversing in Carnforth Station. The train then crosses the main line between Glasgow and London by means of an overbridge, and crosses over a slip road on to the M6 before going underneath the motorway itself. The river which the line keeps running alongside and across at this stage is the River Keer. Soon after, the line bends noticeably to the right, before it passes by the station building at Arkholme. This station was closed many years ago and is now a private dwelling. Its only claim to fame was that a year or two back it featured in the opening sequence of a long-running TV series, when a certain infamous Irishman cleverly disguised as a train-driver, pulled up at the station in a steam-engine, presumably borrowed from the Steamtown Museum at Carnforth, to surprise the owner of Arkholme Station, Jim Bowen of *Bullseye* fame and present him with a certain famous red book.

The train then crosses the River Lune which is very marshy at this point. The only tunnel between Carnforth and Skipton is encountered next before we come to the first station at Wennington. Like all the other intermediate stations, its facilities are fairly basic with just a small brick shelter on both platforms. After Wennington the train passes through the village of Lower Bentham before stopping in the village of Higher Bentham, a mile or so farther on. The station though is simply called 'Bentham'. It has a surprisingly modern-style building on the eastbound platform while a simple stone shelter suffices on the westbound one. Since Wennington, the line has been keeping company with the River Wenning. Ingleborough, a prominent hill, can be seen on the left as Clapham Station – totally unlike a famous junction of the same name – is reached. It is some distance from the village it serves which can also be seen to the left.

After leaving the next station, Giggleswick, the town of Settle can be seen in the distance to the left and soon the famous Settle – Carlisle line descends in from the left to join up with us. The river alongside now is the Ribble, and after Long Preston, a somewhat scattered community, we come to Hellifield. In days gone by this was an important junction station as can be seen from the larger size of its buildings and the ornate iron work beneath the platform canopies. At its east end, a line curves away

The 1.36 p.m. Lancaster–Hull train is stopped at Wennington while the signalman warns the driver of sheep on the line ahead (*Photo:* Tom Heavyside)

to the right. This line is normally freight only and goes via Clitheroe to Blackburn. It is, however, used for DalesRail special trains to Carlisle from Lancashire via Settle. These stop at Clitheroe whose platforms are intact. There are moves afoot to try and persuade British Rail to reopen this line to regular passenger trains and to reopen Clitheroe Station once more. Only time will tell how successful these moves prove to be. As you gaze towards Blackburn from Hellifield though, your attention is also drawn to the bulky mass of Pendle Hill, which is reputed to be the haunt of the Lancashire witches. Gargrave is the only other station encountered before Skipton and it has a pleasant Tudor-style building on the eastbound platform and a small stone shelter on the westbound. Soon we are in Skipton, a pleasant little market town set high up in the hills. It has a castle that is well worth a visit plus a private steam railway featured elsewhere in this book. The station itself is stone built and just outside the town centre, which can be reached by turning right outside the station and going down the hill. Our train is going on to Leeds and, if you are too, then the companion volume to this book *Yorkshire by Rail* will take over describing the scene, for you are now in North Yorkshire.

OXENHOLME–WINDERMERE
by Tim Young and Malcolm Conway

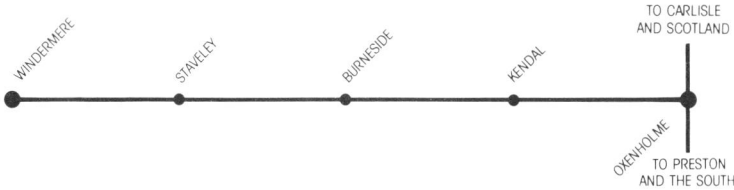

The platform for Carlisle-bound trains at Oxenholme is an island platform, in that there are railway lines running along both sides of it, the one on the far side being the Windermere platform. As the DMU pulls out of the station, it heads north before bending to the left as it clears the end of the platform and descends round a tortuous bend into the valley below, and the town of Kendal. Oxenholme used to be called 'Kendal Junction' but was renamed after a local farm. Kendal, the first stop, is in a very sorry state of repair, vandalised almost to the point of dereliction. Kendal the town, though, is well worth a visit, and is one of the major market towns of the Lake District. Katherine Parr, the sixth wife of Henry VIII and the one who survived, was born here, and Kendal also gives its name to one of the Lake District's most famous delicacies, Kendal Mint Cake. If you have never tasted it, you must try some. Any reputable sweet-shop will sell it and it is not expensive. If you want more details about Kendal, call in at the tourist office at the Town Hall. As we leave, a large goods shed can be seen on the left, though it does not appear to be in railway ownership today. It is, however, a sign of the railway's former prosperity, when wool especially will have been transported all over the country, after starting its journey in that shed. We then cross the River Kent before leaving the town for pleasant Lakeland countryside. On approaching Burneside (pronounced Bernie Side), you cross the only manned level crossing on the line before reaching the station, and if you are alighting here, the platform will be on your right-hand side. At the west end of the station is an ungated level crossing which the train will crawl over at 5 mph, before picking up speed again. There is another level crossing farther on, but this one has automatic barriers operated by the train depressing a treadle on the line when it is a certain distance away.

As we approach Staveley, the looming mass of Hugill Fell in the background dwarfs the tiny village. The line turns so that after leaving Staveley, whose platform is also on the right-hand side, the train runs round the base of the fell, skirts the village of Ings, climbs, leans right, and then drops into Windermere, the teminus of the line. When the line was first envisaged and constructed back in 1847, it was hoped that it would form part of the main line to Scotland but there was strong local opposition to that idea, not least from the poet William Wordsworth, so Windermere became and remains a terminus. Recently the station has been reconstructed, with the main part of the original train shed now housing the Windermere store of a North West supermarket chain, while the station itself, now reduced to a single line as is the entire branch, has a simpler structure. Bowness, one mile from Windermere, is the middle port of call for the Windermere ferries which ply up and down the lake in the summer only. Windermere is the longest lake in England and a pleasant day can certainly be had visiting Ambleside at the northern end and Lakeside with its steam-trains at the southern end by means of these ferries, which used to be owned and operated by Sealink, when a British Rail subsidiary, but are now owned and operated by the Windermere Iron Steamboat Company, under the privatisation arrangements that Sealink underwent a few years ago.

CARLISLE—CARNFORTH VIA BARROW
by Lloyd Daniels, Trevor Garrod and Richard Watts

We leave the Border City by the ex-Maryport & Carlisle Railway route, the first railway promoted entirely in Cumbria. It was the oldest railway to become part of the LMS in 1923. The line leaves Citadel Station parallel with the routes to Lancaster, Newcastle, and the Settle line southwards but soon veers sharply westwards passing the Currock carriage and wagon repair shops which were once the Glasgow & South Western Railway locomotive shed. There is now nothing to indicate that on the opposite side of the line at this point were the M & CR locomotive sheds, demolished in 1930. At Currock Junction the freight line from Bog Junction joins our route as it turns south-westwards; this route was the original M & CR main line to the original terminus at Crown Street.

We soon leave the city behind and pastureland borders the route. We cross the River Caldew and pass the remains of Cummersdale Station, closed in 1951. Dalston Station has changed little although most of the buildings are disused. It is the first of many stations on the Cumbrian Coast line that are request stops—the trains stop to set down passengers if the guard is asked in advance of the station and to pick up passengers if they give a signal to the driver of the train as it approaches. Just after the station there is a fuel storage depot to the south served by a siding. Curthwaite Station was closed in 1950 while Crofton, built as a private station for the Brisco family, was closed much earlier.

The station buildings at Wigton have been removed and replaced with bus-stop shelters. The signal-box here is the first since Carlisle, the area covered by the Carlisle power signal-box extending almost to Wigton. Little remains of the once moderate sized goods facilities although the adjacent factory is still rail-served. At Aikbank Junction the Mealsgate loop of the M & CR diverged southwards. Leegate Station was closed in 1950. Agricultural land gives way to a small area of tree plantations. Just before Brayton Station, closed in 1950, the Solway Junction route diverged northwards. The Caledonian Railway gained access to the area by this route crossing the Solway Firth on a viaduct of 182 30-foot spans. The railway once served a number of collieries from this point onwards towards Maryport, but now it is difficult to find any visible evidence of this once-important source of freight traffic.

Approaching Aspatria the western end of the Mealsgate loop rejoins the main line. The original M & CR signal-box is still in use here. The Dairy Crest creamery dominates land to the south of the station and the bay once used for Mealsgate loop trains, then for rail milk tankers serving the creamery, can be seen although no track remains. A bus-stop shelter is on the westbound platform while the original buildings, mostly disused, still exist on the eastbound platform. At Bulgill the station platforms were staggered either side of the road overbridge. The trackbed of the M & CR Derwent branch to Brigham can be seen climbing away to the south. The line descends into a narrow gorge passing the site of Dearham Bridge Station, closed in 1950, to enter the single platform at Maryport. The headquarters of the M & CR was situated in the station building progressively reduced from 1960 onwards until now there is just a bus-stop shelter. After the road overbridge the M & CR Dock branch diverged northwards and beyond were the company's locomotive works and sheds. Maryport crossing box now guards a road crossing with lifting barriers and as the line turns south-westwards to run along the coast the coal-washery at Risehow is prominent. There are now good views across the Solway Firth to Scotland with the highest peak being Criffel.

We are now on the route of the Whitehaven Junction Railway which became part of the LNWR. Flimby Station is still open. Inland the area was once dotted with collieries which were all rail served but all signs have now disappeared. One of the modern replacement factories is Thames board mills at Siddick for which timber arrives by rail at Workington from Scotland. A short section of the Cleator & Workington Junction Railway remains at Siddick Junction as far as Calva Junction to serve a part of the ex-C & WJR branch to Linefoot for access to the NATO depot at Broughton Moor. Workington Docks can be seen to the west, rail served but little used apart from occasional coal trains. Just before crossing over the River Derwent the site of Derwent Junction and the route to Cockermouth diverging eastwards can still be distinguished. We enter Workington Station, originally known as Workington Main when the C & WJR Central Station still existed.

The station buildings are still complete and were refurbished in 1985. After leaving Workington Station the town is inland and the ex-iron- and steelworks once dominated the coastline. We pass the ex-motive power depot now in use for wagon repairs and then after the new road overbridge the BSC rail rolling mill is on the seaward side. Colourlight signalling introduced in 1984 removed three signal-boxes and resulted in track rationalisation in this area. The Irish Sea comes into view after the works and the Isle of Man is occasionally visible when weather conditions are right. Harrington Station with its low platforms requires the use of steps to detrain. The harbour is now purely used for leisure craft. Soon we are travelling along the sea-wall and the single-line section is nicknamed 'Avalanche Alley' because the unstable colliery tip sometimes slips down on to the line, blocking it and requiring a replacement bus service until it is cleared. At the end of the spoil tip recently landscaped was the locomotive works of Fletcher Jennings, now completely vanished. Parton Station stands on an embankment above the beach and Whitehaven harbour can be seen to the south with St Bees Head beyond. Derelict land inland marks the site of the Lonsdale ironworks and William pit. At Whitehaven Bransty, the new station buildings were opened in December 1981. To the west of Bransty signal box lines lead to docks, disused since 1985.

The single-bore Bransty tunnel takes us directly under the town of Whitehaven to Corkickle Station. Beyond Corkickle no.1 signal box, on the right, is the line from Preston Street goods depot, and from the 'brake'. Until recently, wagons were rope-hauled up the incline to the Marchon works of Albright & Wilson. A once-thriving network of lines around Moor Row left our route to the left; now all track is lifted apart from the disused track to Moor Row.

The line is forced inland by the cliffs around St Bees Head, but rejoins the coast at St Bees Station, continuing through Nethertown and Braystones (where a few years ago a train of bogie tanker wagons left the track and demolished some of the beach houses — fortunately all unoccupied at the time) to Sellafield, where the line from the nuclear plant joins on the left. A triangle was installed here in 1982 for turning steam locomotives on rail-tours using the Cumbrian Coast route. Only three locomotives actually used the triangle before the railtours were discontinued, but it is planned to run them again in summer 1987. A regular traffic in nuclear flasks uses the line into the plant, where a class 08 diesel shunting locomotive hired from BR is used, though the only working industrial steam locomotive in Cumbria is also maintained in operating condition here.

The line continues, now double track again, south-eastwards through Seascale and Drigg (where a siding was recently installed on the right to serve the low-level radioactive dump) before reaching Ravenglass—junction for the famous miniature railway described on page 68. The station buildings on the up side are now in use as a museum.

We cross a viaduct over the river estuary and pass the site of the closed Eskmeals Station. A mile further on are Vickers' gun range sidings on the right. These also include a triangle where steam locomotives used on railtours have been turned in the past. At Bootle, the large house and station buildings are now a private dwelling

A DMU at Seascale on a Barrow–Carlisle train on 6 September 1985 (*Photo:* Tom Heavyside)

separated from the operating station platform; while at Silecroft the station buildings have been demolished and replaced by a bus-stop shelter. Millom Station is also now unstaffed, with the majority of the main building used for an exhibition. Note the Furness Railway ironwork supporting the remaining station canopy. Very little trace can be found of the once-extensive rail system in the area associated with the ironworks.

The railway turns north, skirting the Duddon estuary, reaching Green Road, an 'adopted' station whose smart appearance and well-tended flower beds can be appreciated thanks to the efforts of two local young people. A viaduct takes us over the estuary and then past the scant remains of the former branch to Coniston before we enter Foxfield Station. Note the half-timbered signal box perched high up at the end of the station buildings on the single island platform.

We are now travelling south again through Kirkby-in-Furness and Askam. At Park South Junction the Dalton loop line diverges, allowing trains to avoid Barrow. Very little remains of the once extensive-network of lines in the Barrow area; though there are sidings at the town's station used for storing carriages, locomotives and diesel units while awaiting duties; and lines serving the docks trail in from the right shortly afterwards.

The Furness district was once covered with iron-ore mines, and the Furness Railway, which built the line north and east of Barrow, owed its origins and later its prosperity to iron. The station at Barrow originally had an overall roof, but this was destroyed by enemy action during the Second World War and eventually the whole station was rebuilt by BR. It had been the resting-place for 'Coppernob', an old Furness Railway locomotive which can now be seen at the National Railway Museum in York.

Soon after leaving Barrow Station the line turns north again, almost completing a circle at Dalton Junction, the south-eastern end of the Dalton loop. Beyond Roose, close to the former Furness Abbey Station, was an hotel belonging originally to the Furness Railway and the area was kept as rural as possible with the planting of trees and shrubs round the station building. Both the station and hotel were destroyed by enemy action during the war.

Two short tunnels are passed through and the summit of the line comes shortly after the site of Lindal ore sidings. A locomotive once disappeared into a hole in the ground when the tracks caved into mine workings. Suggestions have been made about a possible recovery and restoration of this locomotive!

At Ulverston is a magnificent example of a Furness Railway Station, completed in 1878 at a cost of £10,000 and built to replace an earlier station opened in 1854 as a terminus of the line from Barrow. The unusual platform arrangement allowed passengers to transfer directly from main line trains to those using the Lakeside branch. At Plumpton Junction, a little further on, the Conishead Priory branch ran off to the right, and a short spur survives to serve the Glaxo chemical works.

The line now crosses the long viaduct over the estuary of the River Leven and runs eastwards towards Cark and Cartmel Station. A short walk from the station is Holker Hall, the former home of the Dukes of Devonshire and now belonging to Mr and Mrs Hugh Cavendish. Many activities take place in the grounds of the Hall such as hot air ballooning, driving trials for horse-drawn carriages and a country show. Leaving Cark and Cartmel Station the line rejoins the waterside at Kents Bank. Kents Bank is famous for the dangerous crossing over the sands to Hest Bank, a distance of 8 miles. Until the railway was built many preferred this route to the alternative 30 mile road trip.

The approach to Grange over Sands Station parallels the promenade. Attractive views can be had across the Morecambe Bay to Arnside and Silverdale as well as to Morecambe and Heysham on a clear day. Grange is a delightful resort largely created

Arnside Station looking towards Silverdale on 4 August 1970 (*Photo:* John Sommerfield)

by the Furness Railway Company in the nineteenth century. Immediately outside the station is an impressive pond, the home of a variety of wild fowl. The town itself is very attractive and walks such as the Hampsfell Nature Trail make it an interesting point for a day out. For those wishing to travel a little further the station is the starting point for a number of bus routes operated by Ribble to places such as Cartmel (for the famous priory) and Haverthwaite (for the steam railway of which more is said later in the book).

Leaving the station the railway stays close to the Morecambe Bay and soon you will see the causeway leading to Holme Island. We now approach the last viaduct on the line which crosses the wide Kent Estuary. The Lakeland Fells can be glimpsed as the train crosses the viaduct. We now arrive at Arnside Station. Arnside is an interesting small town with a promenade and embankment along the Kent estuary which were constructed in 1897. Close to the front is Ye Olde Fighting Cocks, an inn dating from 1660. Walks over the Arnside Knott, a 522-foot-high hill dominating the area, are very rewarding. There is also a nature trail over the Knott and full details can be obtained locally.

The railway passes through some attractive countryside between Arnside and Silverdale. Of note is Arnside Tower, a fifteenth-century pele tower and Middlebarrow quarry on the right and Hawes water, on the left. We now stop at Silverdale. The old station house has been converted into a restaurant. The village is a short way from the station and can be reached by a combination of road and footpath walking in about 20 minutes.

Silverdale is an area full of interest set in some very attractive and unspoilt countryside, providing much to fill a whole day. Immediately outside the station is the RSPB bird reserve at Leighton Moss. Walks around the village can take in the Pepper Pot (on Castlebarrow Head), the cove with its caves, Jenny Brown's Point and the wells at Woodwell and Burton Well. Full details of these and other places of interest can be obtained locally.

From Silverdale the train heads for Carnforth. Again views across the Morecambe Bay can be enjoyed. Very soon we reach Carnforth Station. The town of Carnforth can be used to reach (by Ribble bus) the attractive villages of Warton and Yealand Redmayne as well as Leighton Hall. By the station is the famous Steamtown Railway Museum. You may catch glimpses of the Flying Scotsman and Sir Nigel Gresley locomotives.

The Furness line now joins the West Coast Main line which is described elsewhere in this book.

SETTLE–CARLISLE
by Stan Abbott

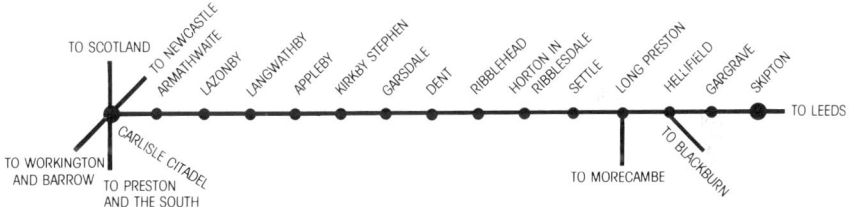

The slow-grinding cogs of the railway judicial process have left the dramatic 72 miles of upland railway linking the North Yorkshire market town of Settle with the Border City of Carlisle standing, at the time of writing, in a 'no man's land', somewhere between the dock and death row.

British Rail, having pronounced the death sentence after years of draining the accused of its very lifeblood in the now-infamous process of 'closure by stealth', awaits the Government's response to the Transport Users' Consultative Committee reports on its case some time in 1987.

The dramatic increase in patronage in 1986 – thanks in no small measure to the reintroduction of local services with local authority backing to stations in the Yorkshire Dales National Park and the Eden Valley – raised hopes of a pre-General Election reprieve and free pardon for the line and its weather-worn 325 bridges, 21 viaducts, and 14 tunnels.

Whether such hopes were well or ill founded may be known before this book is published – what is certain is that whatever the outcome, the story will not be over

29

and that S & C's many supporters will not see this monument to Victorian enterprise and engineering led meekly to the gallows.

The publicity surrounding the closure controversy has taken may travellers over the S & C metals for the first time and many have returned for a second, third, and many more times. For me the S & C is like a vintage movie: the enjoyment is not dulled by each repeated viewing which can guarantee some new 'discovery' – something seen from the carriage window which had escaped my attention through countless trips.

Our journey begins as it did with the Midland Railway engineer James Allport more than 100 years ago, at Settle Junction. The task facing him: to drive an independent route north through some of England's most beautiful yet hostile land, capable of taking express trains at 100 mph.

Settle Junction was, for a short time, a station in its own right but there is little or no evidence remaining today. On a locomotive-hauled train we are soon aware we have joined the S & C as its pace slows perceptibly. We have begun the Long Drag – 15 hard miles at 1 in 100 to Blea Moor with but the briefest respite, which were the Fireman's dread.

On the left, the Carnforth line falls away and bears off and we are soon at Settle proper, an attractive station and former winner of best-kept awards. The S & C's quest for high ground brings it close to the centre of this busy town of about 2,500 people, a rarity on a route where the needs of intermediate communities were a firm second to those of trunk passengers.

We can expect to witness a veritable rush-hour as often scores of trippers join here for the trip over the central 'mountain' section. The line leaves Settle over a massive

A large crowd, indicative of the interest being shown in the line, waiting to join an approaching Carlisle-bound train at Settle on 7 April 1984 (*Photo:* Tom Heavyside)

embankment before we are quickly into the first of many deep cuttings. Look out on the right for the massive Langcliffe Scar with the old Craven Quarry at its foot. Adjacent to the line is probably the finest example of the Hoffman continuous-burning limekiln, a massive structure which it is hoped may be renovated as a tourist attraction.

We are now in the limestone country of the National Park and the 120-yard Taitlands Tunnel marks the North Craven fault, one of a series at the edge of the limestone block through which the River Ribble has carved its course.

The line is threaded through the narrow Stainforth Gorge, a nick point above which the river is slower flowing, crossing two skew viaducts and a section where the engineers diverted the river to make room for the trackbed. At Helwith Bridge are old gravel pits and massive evidence, on the left, of the limestone-quarrying industry. The bed of a former lake gives the briefest stretch of level track.

On our right as we pull into Horton-in-Ribblesdale—the first of eight stations reopened in 1986—is the distinctive Pen y Ghent Hill, one of Yorkshire's famous Three Peaks. On our left is the scar of another massive quarry. The signal-box at Horton is out of commission since a lineside fire started by sparks from the locomotive *Union of South Africa* destroyed cables.

From here the valley continues to open out and the line sticks to a firm limestone footing in contrast to the rolling drumlins to the east which would have made life difficult for the engineers. We pass the reopened Ribblehead Station but do not stop as this is a rare 'one-way' halt, the northbound platform having been removed to make way for new sidings at the former BR ballast railhead. We slow to 30 mph for the crossing of the twenty-four-arch, 100-foot-high Ribblehead Viaduct, the villain in the closure piece.

The ravages of time and one of the harshest climates in the North have combined with the peculiar properties of the limestone blocks from which the viaduct was built to create a major maintenance problem. Estimates of how much it would cost to repair or replace the structure vary widely up to the £7,000,000 replacement cost which BR used to help justify its closure strategy. The single track is now aligned in the centre of the viaduct to minimise loadings on the spandrel walls.

The other great peaks of Ingleborough and Whernside are on our left. Some say that in the right weather you can still occasionally see from the right-hand window foundations of the Batty Wife Hole shanty town to the north of the viaduct which was a miserable home for some of the 6,000-odd navvies who toiled in atrocious conditions to build the line in six years at a cost of £3,500,000—both figures being way above the initial estimates. After crossing the windgap, the line follows across Blea Moor, passing the remote, but still-active signal-box with its passing loops and former overnight quarters for crews. An unusual aqueduct carries Force Gill over the line before we plunge into Blea Moor Tunnel, at 2,629 yards the longest on the line and, at more than 500 feet, also the deepest.

Emerging in to the light of Dentdale, for my money the most beautiful stretch of the line, we cross Dent Head and Arten Gill viaducts, the latter built of the local so-called 'Dent marble'. As we pull into Dent—at 1,100 feet the highest main-line station in England and nearly 5 miles from the village which gives it its name—note the remains of the snow fences on the fellside above us to the right and remember that whole trains have been buried hereabouts in the notorious winters of 1947 and 1963.

Rise Hill Tunnel, some 1,213 yards long, brings us into Garsdale and a near-level stretch where once were the highest water-troughs in the world. At Garsdale Station we can see the route of the old Hawes branch on the right. This has proved by far the most popular of the reopened stations although it is some 6 miles from Hawes.

Now we cross another windgap at the heads of Garsdale and Wensleydale—here the

A steam-hauled Cumbrian Mountain Express special crossing Ribblehead Viaduct on 17 November 1984 (*Photo:* Tom Heavyside)

engineers built Dandry Mire Viaduct in place of the planned embankment because the peat refused to bear the weight of the hardcore.

Two short tunnels—Moorcock and Shotlock Hill—and Lunds Viaduct take us through the post-Glacial landscape into the Ais Gill summit cutting at 1,169 feet where we leave Yorkshire behind and enter the wild country of the Eden's headwaters, with Hellgill on our right and crossing Ais Gill itself on a four-arch viaduct (look out for a pair of characteristic limekilns on the right). Ahead on our left is Wild Boar Fell with Mallerstang Edge to our right.

In the valley below, as we negotiate an extensive and long-standing 'slack', are the ruins of Pendragon Castle, steeped in legend and reputed to be the birthplace of King Arthur.

Birkett Tunnel—at 424 yards the fifth longest on the line—takes us through the Dent fault line and this longest station-less stretch ends at Kirkby Stephen West. The ruling gradient is to thank for placing the station 1½ miles from the little town and 350 feet above it. Note the working signal-box, the well-kept station buildings 'adopted' by the town, the former goods shed now a haulage depot and the railway bungalows on the road to the left.

A couple of miles beyond Kirkby watch on the right—after the turrets of Smardale Hall—for the approach of the old NER line which linked Darlington and Tebay via Stainmore. This passes beneath us as we cross the magnificent Smardale Viaduct—tallest on the line and the last in limestone country—and a careful watch out of the left-hand window will earn a glimpse of the old NER viaduct a mile away.

Saved recently from demolition after a public inquiry it remains in an advanced state of decay – its crumbling piers preview a fate which it is argued could befall those on the S & C if deprived of attention.

Through Crosby Garrett Tunnel, the line bisects the village by the first red sandstone viaduct before entering the deep cutting where the station once stood. As we near the half-way point in our journey we enter the broad plain of the Lower Eden Valley by way of the Helm Beck which we cross by a seven-arch viaduct to join its left bank, cutting through a spur by way of the 571-yard-long Helm Tunnel.

After passing the site of the former Ormside Station we cross the Eden for the first time on the 90 foot-high ten-arch Ormside Viaduct and see on the right the old NER Kirkby Stephen – Penrith line which now serves the Warcop munitions store by way of a retained length from Appleby.

Appleby-in-Westmorland – the historic county town before the 1974 reorganisation saw Westmorland absorbed into Cumbria – is the only staffed station after Settle and, like Settle, it is well kept and a former winner of prizes.

Leaving Appleby, look out on the left for the old Vampire jet in the grounds of the Grammar School which was one of the venues in 1986 for the TUCC hearings into the closure plan. The end of the Warcop branch is on the right as we cross the A66 town bypass before passing below the Roman highway which linked Carlisle and York.

Just past the disused station at the sizable village of Long Marton, look out for the covered conveyor which carries gypsum from a mine to the right of the line to the British gypsum works on the left where we will also see a sizable gypsum quarry.

Then it's through the former station at Newbiggin and across Crowdundle Beck where we can prepare for something rare on the Settle – Carlisle: a level crossing.

Culgaith Station, next to it, remains in reasonable repair, although closed, and the signal-box, like Appleby, remains in commission. Culgaith Tunnel – driven through hard red marl – is at 661 yards the third longest on the line and it is followed by the shallow and much shorter Waste Bank Tunnel.

Our surroundings are now part pastoral, part arable as we pass the broad River Eamont joining the Eden to our left after its journey from Ullswater amid the Lakeland fells, the great bulk of Cross Fell and the Pennines to our right. The topography here is responsible for the occasional turbulent meeting of dissimilar air masses over the Pennines to create the notorious Helm Wind which can certainly break windows and which is reputed to have whisked the coal off firemen's shovels in the good old days.

Soon we are at Langwathby, another reopened station which was – in Midland days – the railhead for a horse-drawn carriage link with the Lake District. Beyond Langwathby we cross the seven-arch viaduct at Little Salkeld where the closed station remains in good condition, before passing the site of the old Long Meg gypsum-mines and their once-extensive sidings on our right. The signal-box is unmanned but maintained in working repair.

Crossing to the left bank of the Eden on the seven-arch red sandstone Eden Lacy Viaduct we can see the start of the Eden Gorge by looking out of the right-hand window. Here – beside the weir – is the site of one of the earliest crossings of the fast-flowing river, while a little farther downstream are Lacy's Caves, carved in the eighteenth century out of the sheer cliff by Samuel Lacy of Salkeld Hall.

Our next stop is at the reopened station at Lazonby and Kirkoswald, after a short tunnel.

In seeking a reasonably straight route, the railway from here keeps clear of the valley bottom while exploiting the general line of the river. The result – thanks also to the instability of much of the rock – is a succession of tunnels, cuttings, and embankments as we cut across spurs and tributary valleys. There are two tunnels at Baron Wood and one just south of Armathwaite where we enter the reopened station after crossing the nine-arch 80 feet-high viaduct at Combe Eden. The village and its castle are below us to the right beside a river crossing which owes its existence to a narrowing of the gorge.

After Armathwaite the line keeps close to the river for about another 4 miles until the disused station at Cotehill where we begin to strike left towards Carlisle, passing the old gypsum-mine and workings at Eden Shales and the closed stations at Cumwhinton and Scotby.

We join the Newcastle – Carlisle Railway – almost forty years older than the S & C – a mile from Citadel Station, a magnificent structure reflecting the glorious days when it was a joint operation involving no fewer than eight companies, each with its own yards and engine shed. After exploring the Border City we can look forward to catching on our return all the sights we missed on the way!

Stan Abbott is the author of *To Kill a Railway*, detailing events leading up to the BR closure plans. He is co-author with Colin Speakman of *Great Walks from the Settle – Carlisle*. Both books are available from Leading Edge Press and Publishing, 1D Rural Workshops, Brunt Acres Road, Hawes, North Yorks, DL8 3PZ. Also available, *Settle & Carlisle Country*, by Alan Earnshaw. Send sae for details.

MANCHESTER VICTORIA – LIVERPOOL LIME STREET
by Andrew Macfarlane

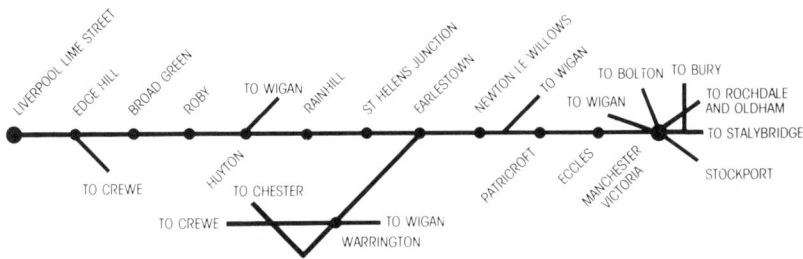

In their publicity for the Settle & Carlisle Railway British Rail claim it to be 'England's Greatest Historical and Scenic Route'. I would like to question the first part of this statement. The line we are about to traverse is certainly a great deal more historic if not nearly so scenic. The Liverpool & Manchester Railway was the world's first 'inter-city'railway specifically designed for use by passengers when it opened on 15 September 1830 – a mere forty-six years before the Settle & Carlisle!

We begin our journey from Platform 11 of Manchester Victoria Station, once the longest platform in Britain. The service to Liverpool is provided either by locomotive-hauled Trans-Pennine trains or by DMUs operating the hourly local service. If we are not in any hurry it will be more rewarding to take one of the local trains as that will enable us to see more of the lineside points of interest.

Our train sets out past the platforms of the former Manchester Exchange Station, closed in May 1969. We can see Manchester Cathedral to our left before we pass Deal Street signal box which dates from LMS days and then Salford Station, mainly used by commuters. Salford only has platforms on the former Lancashire & Yorkshire lines, however, and we pass alongside without stopping. Our train snakes round the 'Salford curves' and the main building of Granada Television is visible to the left. Also to our left we can now see the buildings of Liverpool Road Station, the original terminus of the line. Although it closed to passengers as early as 1844 with the opening of Manchester Victoria, it remained in use for goods traffic until 1975 and the restored buildings are now the home of the Greater Manchester Museum of Science and Industry, including several large railway locomotives built in the Manchester area.

At Ordsall Lane Junction we join the line from Castlefield Junction on the Manchester – Altrincham line and to our right the new 'Windsor Link' is at the time of writing under construction. This short section of line will enable trains from Blackpool and Preston to run into Manchester Piccadilly and beyond to destinations south of the city. Our train now starts to accelerate as we pass to our left the warehouse of Duncan Transrail Ltd. The company receives and dispatches goods by Speedlink freight services and a Government grant was received for the installation of the sidings.

The M602 motorway now runs parallel with us for a while. It was on this section that a spectacular accident occurred in 1984 when a Liverpool – Scarborough express ran into the back of a slow-moving oil train, resulting in an enormous fireball. Amazingly only two people were killed. We pass over the single-track Weaste branch which serves an oil terminal alongside the Manchester Ship Canal. The branch joins us via a junction to our right and to our left is Eccles signal-box, an LMS-built structure. Eccles Station is a basic affair with bus-stop shelters. We are soon at the unstaffed Patricroft Station and to our right are the former Nasmyth Wilson locomotive works, now a Royal Ordnance factory. Immediately after Particroft Station we cross over the Bridgewater Canal which runs from Worsley, a mile north of here, to Runcorn where it joins the Mersey. James Brindley's canal was one of the first in the world when it opened in 1761.

We pass over the M63 motorway which is currently being widened at this point and to our left is Barton Moss Junction signal-box which formerly marked the end of the four-track section from Manchester. Ahead of us lies the infamous Chat Moss which provided no end of problems for George Stephenson, the builder of the line. The Moss is a giant peatbog 5 miles long and 3 miles wide, the depth of the peat varying from 25 to 150 feet. It was drained gradually during the nineteenth century but at the time of the construction of the line was still semi-liquid. The method of construction used was to cut parallel drains leaving a 48-foot strip to dry out and harden. On top of it dried peat and brushwood hurdles were placed. On top of this were put more brushwood, dried heather, and hurdles and on top of that earth, sand, and gravel. Finally a thick layer of cinders was laid down which carried the wooden sleepers for the rails. However, in some places tipping could go on for three months with nothing to show for it. Eventually the technique did work and so the line was carried on what was effectively a 'floating mattress'. Incredibly this section of the line proved to be one of the cheapest to construct, the final cost being a mere £27,500!

Astley signal-box to our left is a modern structure controlling a level crossing. It is the 'fringe' box to Warrington power signal-box which controls our route as far as Rainhill. Our train soon passes the village of Glazebury and the scenery becomes more agricultural. Not long afterwards we see to our right a large wedge-shaped expanse of open land. This was the former Kenyon Junction Station where the line from Bolton Great Moor Street once joined our line. The station closed in 1961 but the recent massive growth of Culcheth less than a mile to the south would make it a good candidate for reopening.

At Parkside East Junction a spur leaves to our right to join the West Coast main line and soon on our left is the well-kept memorial to William Huskisson, MP for Liverpool who was possibly the first person to be killed by a moving passenger train. The accident happened on the opening day of the line when Huskisson went to speak

35

to the Duke of Wellington who was seated in a train. He failed to get out of the way of the *Rocket* which was approaching on the adjacent line and his left leg was run over and badly mutilated. He was carried to Eccles aboard the locomotive *Northumbria*, driven by George Stephenson himself, but died later of his injuries.

Overhead wires now appear above us as we approach Parkside West Junction, the other side of the triangular junction. We pass under the M6 motorway and to our left is Parkside Colliery which provides considerable traffic for the railway in the shape of 'merry-go-round' coal trains to Fiddlers Ferry power station. Beneath us is the West Coast main line as we arrive at Newton-le-Willows Station which still retains its original buildings. To our right as we enter the station are the sidings of the Richard Lawson Car Delivery Group which receive new cars for distribution in the North West.

A short hop brings us to Earlestown Station, originally known as Newton Junction. At Earlestown East Junction the overhead wires follow the Warrington line. Electric trains only pass this way if there is a blockage on the West Coast main line between Winwick and Golborne junctions. Earlestown is a triangular station although the west–south curve is no longer used regularly by passenger trains. Note the original Liverpool & Manchester Tudor-style waiting-room on the Liverpool-bound platform.

Shortly after Earlestown we cross one of the most famous engineering structures on the line, the Sankey Viaduct, which formerly carried the line over the Sankey Canal, now filled in at this point. The impressive viaduct consists of nine arches made of brick with stone facings. Each arch has a span of 50 feet and the underside of each arch was 60 feet above the water-level of the canal to enable boats with tall masts to pass underneath.

The next landmark is the former Bold Colliery which closed in 1985 and is at the time of writing being demolished. Beyond it is Bold power station. The sidings adjacent to the main line became famous during the celebrations to mark the 150th anniversary of the line in 1980 when they were used for stabling the locomotives used in the cavalcades. St Helens Junction is now the most important station on the line, being served by InterCity and local trains. The main building on the Manchester-bound platform is of London & North Western Railway origin and dates from the 1860s.

Immediately beyond the station the branch to St Helens Central, now freight only, diverges to the right and we pass under the line from St Helens to Widnes, now only open as far as Sutton Manor Colliery. This line has an interesting history, having opened only two years after our line, in 1832, mainly to convey coal from the St Helens area to the docks on the banks of the Mersey. It originally included an inclined plane complete with stationary engine immediately to the south of the bridge over our line.

The next station is probably the most famous of all. Every schoolboy has heard of the Rainhill Trials prior to the opening of the line which were, of course, won by Robert Stephenson's *Rocket*. Other competitors were Timothy Hackworth's *Sans Pareil*, Braithwaite and Ericsson's *Novelty*, Timothy Burstall's *Perseverance*, and Thomas Brandreth's *Cycloped*, the last a highly bizarre entry consisting of a horse on a moving platform! As we enter the station on the right is the London & North Western Railway signal-box. The station buildings are typical L & NW and date from the 1860s. The trials are commemorated by a sign on the Manchester-bound platform and at the end of the platforms is the famous Skew Bridge which carries the A57 over the railway. It was probably the first bridge ever to cross over a railway at an angle, the angle of skew being 34 degrees and the bridge remains in virtually its original condition.

A couple of miles beyond Rainhill, at Huyton Quarry, we see to our left the connection to Cronton Colliery, now disused. At Huyton Junction we are joined from the right by the line from St Helens Central and arrive at Huyton, a busy suburban station and bus–rail interchange. Note the fine semaphore junction signal at the end of the Manchester platform. An L & W signal-box stands at the opposite end of the same platform. Very soon we are at Roby which retains its L & NW building on the Liverpool platform. Broad Green Station was rebuilt in 1972 to make way for the M62 motorway. A very short siding on our right serves a warehouse of W. H. Smith & Son Ltd.

A short distance farther on we enter the spectacular Olive Mount cutting which was hewn from the solid rock by hand in the days before mechanical aids. It is 70 feet deep and was originally only 20 feet wide, being widened in 1871 when the line was quadrupled as far as Huyton Quarry. Olive Mount Junction signal-box, an L & NW structure, controls the eastern arm of the triangular junction with the Bootle branch, the western arm of which trails in shortly afterwards. This is now mainly used by Freightliner trains to and from the Royal Seaforth Docks.

We are joined from the left by the main line from London Euston and arrive at Edge Hill Station, the 1836 buildings of which were restored as part of the 150th anniversary celebrations. The original terminus of the line was at Crown Street just beyond Edge Hill, no trace of which remains today. Our train enters Lime Street cutting for the final leg of the journey. This was originally a tunnel when Lime Street opened in 1836 but was subsequently mostly opened out. Our journey ends under the overall roof of Liverpool's principal station, 31¾ miles from Manchester Victoria, after nearly an hour's travelling over what is undoubtedly one of the most fascinating railways in the world.

Further Reading
David Singleton, *Liverpool and Manchester Railway – A mile by mile guide to the world's first 'modern' railway* (Dalesman Books 1975).
Geoffrey O. Holt *A Regional History of the Railways of Great Britain,* Volume 10 *The North West* (David & Charles 1978).
John Marshall *Forgotten Railways – North-West England* (David & Charles 1981).

EARLESTOWN – WARRINGTON BANK QUAY
by Andrew Macfarlane

Trains from Earlestown to Warrington Bank Quay form part of the service from Manchester Victoria to Chester and North Wales and run at roughly hourly intervals. Our train will either be made up of locomotive-hauled carriages or one of the new Sprinter diesel multiple-units which were introduced on the line in May 1986. The line on which we are about to travel is of great historical interest, having formed part of two of the first long-distance main line routes in Britain. It was opened by the Warrington & Newton Railway as early as 1831 and was engineered by Robert Stephenson, its first locomotives *Warrington, Newton,* and *Vulcan* also being Stephenson-built. As from July 1837 the line formed the final section of the Grand Junction Railway's main route from Birmingham to the Liverpool & Manchester Railway at Newton Junction (as Earlestown was known until 1861), which was opened to connect the Midlands with both Northern cities. It soon after also became part of the main West Coast route, a role the southern section of the line still fulfils, the section from Earlestown to Winwick Junction having been bypassed by the Winwick Junction to Golborne Junction cut-off line, opened in 1864. The line from Winwick Junction to Golborne Junction via Earlestown and Newton-le-Willows was, however, electrified with the West Coast main line in the early 1970s and is used as a diversionary route when the direct line is blocked.

We depart from one of the sharply curving platforms on the east – south side of the triangular junction at Earlestown and the single-track west – south curve joins from the right. We traverse a shallow cutting and soon pass to our left the historic Vulcan Foundry which began manufacturing steam locomotives in 1830. The great Daniel

Gooch, later Sir Daniel Gooch, of the GWR was apprenticed here in 1834 and the works soon acquired a reputation for exporting its products all over the world, especially to India, America, Russia, and Japan. The home market also provided many orders and a large number of the Stanier Black Five 4-6-0s were built here between the wars. In 1955 the firm was taken over by English Electric and built many BR diesel-electric locomotives including the famous Deltics for the East Coast main line. The works remain open although they no longer produce locomotives. Adjacent to the works is Vulcan village, an interesting example of a self-contained nineteenth-century community. It was served by a wooden-platformed halt until the 1960s.

We descend to join the West Coast main line at Winwick Junction and the route becomes four track. We pass through open country and to our left is the rather foreboding Winwick Hospital which specialises in cases of mental illness. To our right we are running roughly parallel with the disused St Helens Canal. We pass under the M62 motorway and to our left is the Winwick Quay industrial area. The original terminus of the Warrington & Newton Railway was in Dallam Lane, Warrington, over to our left but we continue past the Warrington freight terminal to our left, opened in 1983 to replace the goods depot at Warrington Central, and pass under the Cheshire Lines Manchester–Liverpool line before arriving at Warrington Bank Quay Station, 4½ miles from Earlestown. The station was opened by the Grand Junction Railway in 1837 and the town centre is over to our left, the fine Town Hall with its Corinthian columns being only a short walk away.

SOUTHPORT–LIVERPOOL CENTRAL
by Tim Young

Southport is one of the North West's three major coastal resorts and also a major dormitory town for Liverpool. As such it enjoys a fast and frequent electric service so we will join one of these trains as it stands in one of the right-hand bays. Southport Station, though, is a little unusual as it has had a shopping arcade built round it. Our train is about to leave, so we'll hop on board before the automatic doors slide shut. As we glide out, the train snakes round to the right and then picks up speed. As semi-detached suburbia passes by, we soon reach the first stop at Birkdale. After Birkdale, more suburbia passes till the next station at Hillside. This stretch of coastline is also good golfing country, and this station was the nearest station to the course used in the 1983 British Open, the last time that championship was played in the Southport area. Golf soon becomes the order of the day and we pass courses right and left. Houses though return once more as we approach Ainsdale, a typical commuter station with a few shops by it and a large car park full of vehicles. As we leave we have yet more houses to our left with woodland to our right. While the woodland remains, the houses soon disappear to make way for a small airfield. Freshfield Station is the next stop on the outskirts of Formby and after another short trip through suburbia, Formby Station itself. Between Ainsdale and Formby, until recently, an area of marshland known as 'The Slacks' just behind the dunes on the coast, was the only British habitat of the Natterjack Toad. A new housing development in Ainsdale caused the marshland to be drained and the toad population was decimated and is now confined to certain small protected areas. We then venture briefly into open countryside with coastal dunes on the skyline at our right, though we never glimpse the sea. Soon a forces training camp is on the right before Hightown Station brings more houses with it.

We then see houses to our right and fields to the left before one final spell in the country. We then pass the West Lancashire Golf Club's course on our right before coming to Hall Road Station with its depot behind it on the right. Blundellsands and Crosby is the next station and after that the island platform of the other Waterloo Station on BR. By now the housing has become less affluent as we approach Liverpool. We soon pass Seaforth and Litherland Station and then the cranes and derricks of Liverpool Docks on the right skyline. The docks stretch for quite a distance and there is a rail link serving part of them. Our next stop is at Bootle New Strand and after that office blocks seem to abound as we then come to Bootle Oriel Road. One of our best-known national institutions, National Girobank, has its main headquarters in Bootle. After the next stop at Bank Hall we are joined on our left by the lines from Ormskirk and Kirkby before Sandhills is reached. After that we go underground first to Moorfields, built adjacent to the site of the former Liverpool Exchange Station and finally into Liverpool Central. Like the northern terminus at Southport, Liverpool Central has had a shopping arcade built round it and once through the barriers, you are in a light and airy shopping piazza. If, however, you want to sightsee the Liverpool Tourist Information Bureau would be pleased to help you, being just five minutes' walk away.

LIVERPOOL CENTRAL–PRESTON VIA ORMSKIRK
by Geoffrey Nelson

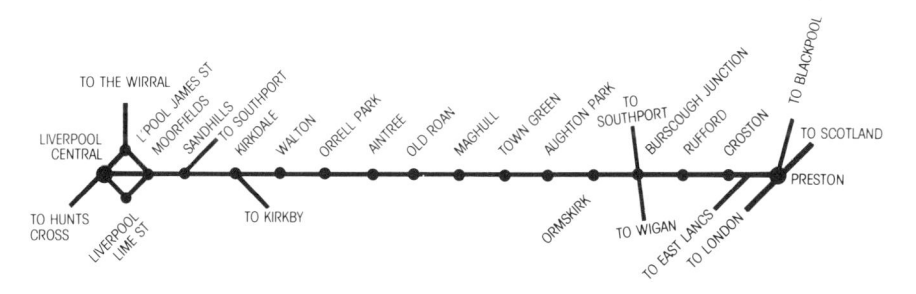

Leading off a shopping arcade with a pleasing glass roof in Ranelagh Street is Liverpool Central Station. The first stage of our journey, to Ormskirk on Merseyrail's Northern line, leaves from an underground island platform. Leaving Central Station, the train runs through a tunnel formerly used by Wirral-bound trains, but at Paradise Junction beneath Church Street and Whitechapel, the Northern line swings sharply to the right, and the train rushes through new tunnelling to Moorfields which replaced Exchange Station in 1977. Climbing out of the tunnel, up to a viaduct which carries the line to Sandhills, you can catch glimpses of the Mersey and Wirral shore, the docks, and the massive Stanley Dock Tobacco Warehouse, the floor space of which is said to cover about 36 acres. Along this stretch of line much demolition of property has occurred in recent years, including Tate & Lyle's premises. The parking area, to be seen on the right, is now used by Crosville buses before the Leeds and Liverpool Canal is crossed for the first time. After Sandhills, the train heads for Kirkdale, alighting point for Liverpool and Everton football fans.

The Southport line curves sharply to the left. We pass beneath Stanley Road bridge, and run alongside Kirkdale sidings with the depot in the background. Then the train traverses two long tunnels and if you look up on the right, after leaving the second tunnel, you may observe Walton Hospital's clock tower. The Kirkby line sweeps to the right, before we pass Walton signal box, and swing into Walton Station. The prison may be glimpsed to the left, and its forbidding wall looks down on the train as it covers the short distance to Orrell Park. Housing and vegetation line the way to Aintree. We pass over the cutting which once carried the route from Aintree to what is now Southport's Lord Street Bus Station. The neglected platform on the left is used by specials from Bootle on Grand National Day. The way to Old Roan is along an embankment. To the right, running parallel, is the A59 to Preston, the Grand National grandstand, and Vernon's Pools premises before the Leeds and Liverpool canal is crossed again and we enter Old Roan Station, named after the nearby pub.

We cross the A59 and begin the downhill run to Maghull passing over the M57. Crossing the narrow River Alt and the M58, we see Sefton Church on the left in the distance and, to the right, high-rise flats at Kirkby. The line rises over the canal for a third time, before Maghull Station which has a signal box and continental-style level crossing, the only one on the line before Ormskirk. Leaving Maghull, we pass beneath Poverty Lane bridge. The train passes beneath two bridges and through a cutting. Leaving it, the walls of Park Lane High Security Hospital are on the right. Fields stretch away on both sides of our embankment; distant Lydiate is on the left; and a signal box is passed before Town Green Station. A cutting takes the line uphill to Aughton Park, then a downhill run brings us to a bridge, once past which Ormskirk spreads out on both sides of the track. To the right, beyond fields and houses, can be seen Edge Hill College and, farther away still, the mushroom-shaped water-tower at Scarth Hill. Housing is on both sides as we approach a deep, black stone cutting. Once under Moor Street Bridge, we swing on to a single track, entering the station beneath Derby Street Bridge, with the Methodist church looking down.

The Preston train stands at the north end of Ormskirk's single platform. The train is a Pacer unit, with an eye-catching two shades of blue and white livery. Some are painted in Greater Manchester's orange, brown and white livery, and thus nicknamed 'Jaffa cakes'. The driver has a token which he will hand in at Rufford. Most of the line to Preston is single track, and the token safeguards the train while using it. On the right is the car park. Once the 'Skem Jazzer' stood there, waiting to leave for Skelmersdale and Rainford Junction, but the tank engine and two coaches have gone for good. We're off! On the right the water-tower in Tower Hill can be seen. Greetby Hill School is plainly visible, while the rough ground nearer the train once held carriage sidings and an engine shed. The quaint squat building in the middle of the field on our right is a folly called 'Bath Lodge'. It was built as a shooting-lodge on the Lathom estate, probably in the middle of the eighteenth century. There is plenty of arable land on this route. The two stone pillars on the right, by trees and caravans, belonged to Burscough Priory. When Henry VIII dissolved it, its bells were taken to Ormskirk and hung in the parish church tower. We come to a succession of five bridges before we reach Burscough Junction. We are hoping that a halt may be opened along here to cater for the Mill Dam Lane area. Some of the houses peep over the top of the cutting. On the left are the grounds of Lordsgate School. Burscough Junction has a

40

very long platform. In the days of through main line trains from Liverpool it seemed unnecessarily long, now it is ridiculous! Then, on the left, are Ainscough's impressive mill premises before our old friend, the Leeds and Liverpool Canal is crossed again. We'll meet it again in a few minutes. The disconnected track on the left runs down to Burscough Bridge. Trains to Southport went down there until March 1962. Beneath us is the Southport–Wigan line. The embankment coming up to meet us could carry a track once more. Then trains from Preston would run to Burscough Bridge to meet electric trains from Liverpool via Ormskirk. Parbold Hill can be clearly seen on the right, with more hills beyond, including Winter Hill with its television mast.

The A59, having been visible on and off since Ormskirk, comes closer on our left. The road meanders somewhat while much of the railway between Burscough and Midge Hall is in a straight line. There are two bridges ahead; the brickwork and concrete foundations you can see down to the right just before the second one were associated with the tank that supplied the water troughs used by steam engines. Crossing the Leeds and Liverpool Canal's Lower Douglas Navigation, flowing obliquely beneath the railway, and passing trees which line the track on either side, the water comes quite close to the railway on the left and we shall see a lock. Just to the left of the bridge with the vivid blue railings which spans the water is Rufford Church, St Mary's. We have now entered Rufford Station. The signalman comes to take the token from the driver in exchange for one which will enable us to proceed to Midge Hall. On the right is the only passing loop between Ormskirk and Preston. The level crossing, one of two between Ormskirk and the outskirts of Preston, is the old 'swing-gates' type. We then cross the recently widened River Douglas. On the left in the mass of trees is Rufford Old Hall, built by the Hesketh family in the fifteenth century and given to the National Trust in 1936. The A59 makes for Sollom and Tarleton, you may be able to see Tarleton Church in the distance. On this stretch of line there are several unmanned crossings. A metal plate displaying 'W' tells the driver

A Pacer unit approaching Rufford on a service from Preston to Ormskirk on 28 May 1986 (*Photo:* Tom Heavyside)

when to sound his horn. The tall chimney ahead on the right means that we are nearly at Croston.

Ahead of us is an impressive bridge with prominent railings curving gracefully over the track. Once over the River Yarrow, we come to extensive modern housing on our right, on the left are the remains of a disused brickworks. This is the only station between Ormskirk and Preston where the platform is on the right. Members of the Ormskirk–Preston Travellers' Association have put a lot of time and effort into sprucing up the station. The Station House has been refurbished by a new owner and looks cared for. Quite a few people usually join the train at Croston. We cross a narrow stretch of water then trees and fields make up the scenery. On the right an extension to Wymott Prison is being built where a wartime Royal Ordnance factory used to be. We slow down at Midge Hall so the driver can hand the token to the signalman. The continental-style road crossing here has arms which rise skywards when the train has gone. We accelerate past Midge Hall's closed station. Some day, maybe, trains will call here again. On the left are distant hills while on the right is Leyland and part of the British Leyland empire. We come to a long curve to the right, then a long straight stretch before we swing left to run downhill. At the end of this stretch the train slows down and gingerly makes its way across a new bridge. To the right, a new road approaches from Leyland to continue to Penwortham on the left. The scenery here will soon be altered. At Moss Lane Junction the train turns left. It used to be possible for trains to carry on to Lostock Hall, but there is no track that way now. We begin to run downhill beneath two shabby bridges. The tracks on the right on a higher level carry trains to and from Blackburn, East Lancashire and Leeds. Two more shabby bridges then we move carefully on to the Blackburn line at Farington Curve Junction and the overhead wires tell us that we are about to join the West Coast main line from London to Glasgow.

Now there are four tracks side by side. We are in a wide cutting. Just ahead is a bridge, and another one, called 'Skew Bridge', because of the angle at which it crosses the railway. The third bridge we pass under carries heavy piping. Freight lines are on the left. We emerge from the cutting quite high up. Down on the left is Penwortham with quite an assortment of commercial premises and housing. Ahead to the left is St Walburge's Church, built in 1852, with a spire over 300 feet high. It was designed by J. Hansom, inventor of the Hansom cab – quite a versatile character. On a distant hill to the right, hidden by trees, is Hoghton Tower, built by Thomas Hoghton 1562–65, and restored during the last century. The distinctive hill farther back is Pendle Hill, dropping steeply on its left, and home of the Lancashire Witches. Bouncing over points like a tram in motion, we cross the River Ribble. Preston's agreeable skyline is on the right. The bridge on the right used to carry Ormskirk and Blackburn trains into Preston by the 'back way'. The park on the right is Miller Park, overlooked by the former Park Hotel. At its foot, by the black brickwork, used to be a sizeable signal-box. On the left, modern Royal Mail premises are to be seen as we enter the station.

WIGAN–LIVERPOOL CENTRAL VIA KIRKBY
by Andrew Macfarlane

Trains leave Wigan Wallgate for Kirkby (pronounced Kirby) every hour, although there are no trains at the time of writing in the evening or on Sundays. The line was once part of the Lancashire & Yorkshire Railway main line from Manchester to Liverpool but has now become something of a backwater. If ever a line were crying out for the formation of a rail users' group, it is this one! We depart from Wallgate and almost immediately pass under the West Coast main line. The Southport line diverges to the right and also to the right is the concrete 1930s' Wigan Wallgate signal box. We soon cross over the Leeds and Liverpool Canal and then the River Douglas. The Pemberton loop line formerly joined from the left before the station of the same name which, like all of the stations on the line, has bus-stop shelters. We pass under the M6 motorway and arrive at Orrell Station, situated in a leafy cutting, after which we pass through Upholland Tunnel, 959 yards long, the summit of the line and its most significant engineering feature. We enter a cutting before Upholland Station and there are views over open country before Rainford Station, formerly Rainford Junction, which boasts the only signal-box on the line, a London Midland & Scottish Railway structure. Branches formerly ran from here to Ormskirk via Skelmersdale and St Helens via Crank, both of which closed to passengers in the 1950s and to freight in the 1960s. Both lines are walkable, the St Helens line being the more interesting. From Rainford Junction it runs on an embankment to Rainford village and from there to the former Rookery Station has been made into the Rainford Linear Park.

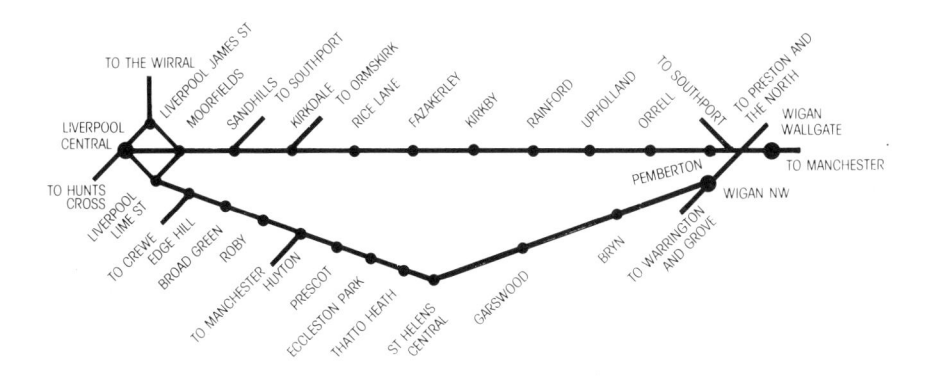

Our driver takes the token for the now-singled section on to Kirkby which has taken on something of the character of a rural branch with weeds growing between the rails in places. Housing on either side of the line heralds our arrival at Kirkby, 12¼ miles from Wigan. Kirkby is a large housing estate on the edge of Liverpool and we change here to a Merseyrail electric train for the remainder of our journey. There is no physical connection between the two lines at Kirkby. A new station building was provided when the line was electrified in 1977. After a short wait our train accelerates away quietly and we pass over the M57 motorway. To our right are the Fazakerley permanent way sidings before we arrive at Fazakerley Station. The next station, Rice Lane, was until recently known as 'Preston Road' and retains some of its original buildings on the Liverpool-bound platform. To our right is the Lancashire & Yorkshire Walton Junction signal-box as we join the line from Ormskirk. We pass through Kirkdale Nos. 1 and 2 tunnels which are respectively 493 and 210 yards long. Kirkdale is the next stop and we note the depot for the Merseyrail electric trains to our right before the Southport line joins from the right. To our right also we can see Liverpool Docks and we cross over the Leeds and Liverpool Canal for the second time before Sandhills Station, and island platform whose name is no longer an accurate description of its surroundings! We dive down to Moorfields Station on the Liverpool Link line, opened in 1977. Our former terminus was Liverpool Exchange and the restored frontage of that station survives to conceal a modern redevelopment scheme. Liverpool Central Low Level is the present terminus of our train from Kirkby.

43

LIVERPOOL LIME STREET–WIGAN VIA ST HELENS CENTRAL
by Andrew Macfarlane

The service on the line we are about to travel on was significantly improved as from September 1986 thanks to welcome additional finance from Merseyside Passenger Transport Executive, and the timetable for 1986–87 showed three trains an hour between Liverpool Lime Street and St Helens Central, two of those running through to Wigan North Western and one continuing on to Preston. The whole of the line was once part of the London & North Western Railway. Our train will be formed of one of the new Pacer units and we will probably make our exit from Lime Street Station via a curious single-track tunnel to the left of the remainder of the main lines. The Preston trains form a semi-fast service and do not serve all stations; the other trains, however, call at every intermediate station.

We diverge from the Manchester Victoria line beyond Huyton Station and travel on a high embankment before crossing over the M57 motorway. There is a shallow cutting before Prescot Station, which is served by all trains. Note the original station building on the St Helens platform. To our right is a London & North Western Railway signal-box and to the left the siding connection into the British Insulated Callander Cables factory. We pass through a cutting before Eccleston Park Station, situated in leafy surroundings, which retains its L & NW building on the Liverpool platform. We next traverse a deep rock cutting, which in summer is lined with ferns and enter a short tunnel before Thatto Heath Station, the wooden buildings of which are still in good condition. After a cutting with sloping sides we are flanked on both sides by the main works of Pilkingtons Ltd and the freight-only line from St Helens Junction joins from the right immediately before St Helens Central Station, which was rebuilt in the 1960s. The town of St Helens has a population of 102,000 and can trace its origins to a chapel dedicated about 1540 to St Helen. Coal-mining was initially its main industry and glass-making is thought to have begun in 1696. The area can lay claim to the first canal in England in the Sankey Brook Navigation, which opened in 1757.

A two-car diesel multiple-unit in Olive Mount cutting just outside Lime Street Station on a Liverpool Lime Street–Wigan train on 22 August 1970 (*Photo:* John Sommerfield)

The chemical industry became important in the eighteenth century and the nineteenth saw a rapid growth in the town's population. Today the name St Helens is synonymous with glass and Pilkingtons are the largest employers although the chemical and coal industries remain significant. The Glass Museum at Pilkingtons main factory details the fascinating history of the industry and is well worth a visit.

To our left as we leave St Helens are sidings for the BR Chief Civil Engineer's department and to the right an L & NW signal box, formerly St Helens No. 2, the 'fringe' to Warrington power signal-box, which also controls the Wigan area. We soon see to our left the Cowley Hill works of Pilkington's. We cross a viaduct and note several overbridges which have been attractively painted in two shades of green. Garswood Station is served only by the hourly Wigan trains and retains its distinctive original buildings in grey brick with stone window-surrounds. We cross from Merseyside into Greater Manchester and pass over the M6 motorway before Bryn Station, where the buildings are similar to those at Garswood though on a smaller scale. Bryn serves the large residential area of Ashton-in-Makerfield over to our right. Farther on, on the right-hand side, is the Three Sisters recreation area before we cross over the Leigh branch of the Leeds and Liverpool Canal. On our left are now the barren wastes of Ince Moss, where spent railway ballast is tipped. At Ince Moss Junction a freight-only spur curves round to the right to join the West Coast main line at Bamfurlong Junction. We join the WCML at Springs Branch Junction opposite the motive power depot and run into Wigan North Western Station, the buildings of which date from electrification of the main line in the early 1970s.

LIVERPOOL CENTRAL – HUNTS CROSS VIA ST MICHAELS
by Andrew Macfarlane

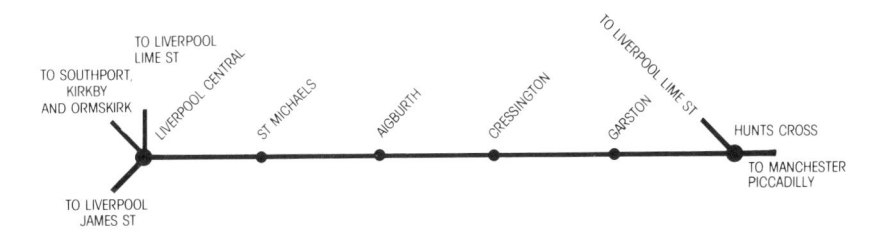

The story of this line is one of a phoenix-like revival after apparent final closure. Until September 1966 our route formed part of the main line from Liverpool Central to Manchester Central of the former Cheshire Lines Committee. From that date, however, the Manchester trains were diverted into Liverpool Lime Street Station and only the Liverpool – Gateacre local service remained on this section until it finally succumbed in April 1972. Thereafter most of the line was used only by an occasional train from Brunswick oil terminal, 1½ miles from Liverpool Central. Liverpool Central Station itself was demolished even before the withdrawal of the Gateacre service and the other stations became increasingly derelict. However, Merseyside Passenger Transport Executive had plans for such a useful suburban route and the line was electrified with a third rail and incorporated in the Liverpool Link project, the Liverpool Central Low Level to Garston section reopening in 1978. The section from Garston to Hunts Cross was reactivated in 1983.

Our train will have probably come from Southport and will be one of the modern Class 507 or 508 electric multiple-units. Trains leave Liverpool Central for Hunts Cross every fifteen minutes in off-peak hours and every half-hour on Sundays. We depart and emerge from the Link tunnel only to pass through the four St James tunnels, all of which are about 200 yards long. We curve round to the left at the site of the former Brunswick locomotive depot and pass through Dingle Tunnel (1,082 yards long) to emerge into a cutting before St Michaels Station, our first stop. This was the nearest station to the 1984 Liverpool Garden Festival and new platform approach ramps were provided here by Marks & Spencer PLC in view of the similarity of the station name to their trade mark. The CLC street-level building was renovated for the festival. Most of the site of the Garden Festival remains open as the Festival Gardens. St Michaels Tunnel (103 yards long) follows before we traverse another cutting and enter Fulwood Tunnel (200 yards long) where we pass the disused platforms of Otterspool Station, closed in 1951. The next station, Aigburth, was known as 'Mersey Road and Aigburth' until 1972. The short Grassendale Tunnel (76 yards long) follows before Cressington Station, which was restored to its former glory in time for its reopening and won awards from Europa Nostra and the Civic Trust. Note the former gas lamps converted to electric. Beyond Cressington a freight-only connection to Speke Junction on the Crewe–Liverpool line diverged until 1977. We curve to the left and arrive at Garston Station, a bus–rail interchange situated in leafy surroundings. The 62-yard long Woolton Tunnel follows, and we pass under the main Euston–Liverpool line before we join the Liverpool Lime Street–Manchester Piccadilly line at Hunts Cross West Junction. Hunts Cross, 7¼ miles from Liverpool Central, is our terminus. An hourly connecting service runs from here to Manchester Oxford Road, calling at all stations and there is a welcome proposal to extend the third rail electrification to Hough Green which is the next station towards Manchester.

MANCHESTER VICTORIA–WIGAN VIA ATHERTON
by Andrew Macfarlane

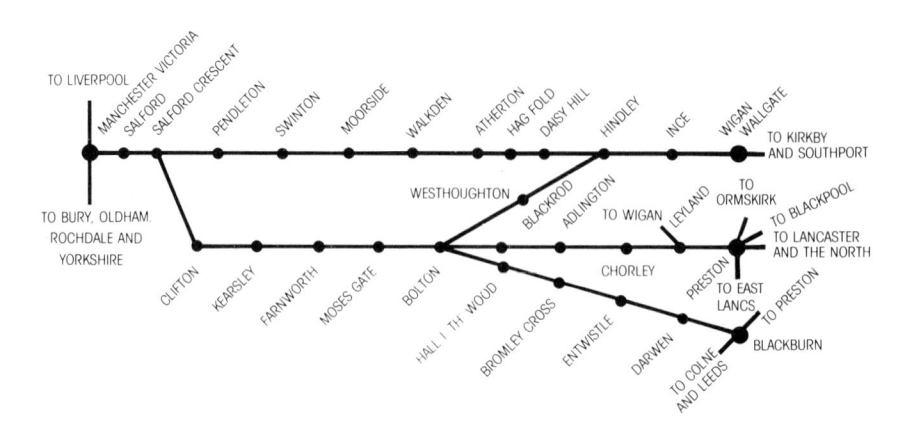

The service from Manchester to Wigan via Atherton is basically hourly on Mondays to Saturdays but there are no trains on Sundays. We depart from one of the through platforms at Victoria and our first stop is Salford. The new station at Salford Crescent, opened in May 1987, is the second port of call. We immediately diverge from the Bolton line at Windsor Bridge Junction on to the former Lancashire & Yorkshire main line to Liverpool, opened in 1888. We are very soon at the island platform of Pendleton Station, formerly Pendleton Broad Street, which retains its canopy to shelter waiting passengers. After Pendleton we curve sharply to the left at Brindle Heath Junction. The line straight ahead to Agecroft Junction was closed in May 1987. As we climb a 1 in 80 gradient we pass Agecroft Colliery to our right. The two running lines diverge round the site of the island platforms at Irlams o' th' Height and Pendlebury and we pass through one of the Pendlebury tunnels, which are 201 yards long.

Swinton is our next stop and the Rugby League Ground can be seen to the right as we approach. The platform canopy and street-level buildings survive. We are soon at Moorside, formerly Moorside and Wardley, and then pass under the M62 motorway. As we slow for Walkden Station we note the Lancashire & Yorkshire signal-box to our left. The island platform here also retains its canopy. There were formerly water-troughs near Walkden where steam locomotives could replenish their tenders at speed. We pass over the trackbed of the former London & North Western Railway Manchester–Bolton line and to our left have a good view over open country towards Chat Moss. Atherton, formerly Atherton Central, is another island platform with canopy. Atherton goods yard signal-box to our left is a BR standard structure. The line threads a residential area and a new station, Hag Fold, opened there in May 1987. We arrive at the delightfully named Daisy Hill Station, once more an island platform. A little farther on we reach the former Dobbs Brow Junction where a cut-off line diverged to the right. This ran to Red Moss Junction on the Bolton–Preston line and was until 1968 used by rush-hour trains between Manchester and Blackpool avoiding Bolton.

At Crow Nest Junction we are joined from the right by the line from Lostock Junction, Bolton. The signal box dates from the early 1970s and is the 'fringe' to Warrington power signal box. We soon arrive at Hindley Station, formerly Hindley North. Note the Lancashire & Yorkshire mural to our left depicting a $2-4-2$ tank engine, a type used on many suburban services. Moving on, we cross over the former Whelley line, which formed an avoiding line round Wigan for the West Coast main line and was extensively used during electrification work in the early 1970s. It was taken out of use in 1974. Shortly afterwards the former Pemberton loop line diverged to the left. This was used by express trains between Manchester and Liverpool, avoiding Wigan. It joined the Wigan Wallgate–Liverpool line before Pemberton Station. Ince is another island platform which has a bus-stop shelter. We run alongside the West Coast main line past Wigan North Western Station and dive down to Wigan Wallgate. The island platform has been modernised by Greater Manchester Passenger Transport Executive although the fine L & Y street-level building and canopy survive.

Wigan with a population of 90,000 has a history dating back to pre-Roman times. The name 'Wigan' is Celtic in origin and the Romans knew it as 'Coccium', a small fort guarding a road junction beside the River Douglas. The town was granted a Royal Charter in 1246 and its market, tracing its origins back to the thirteenth century, today takes place on Mondays and Fridays. There has been a place of worship on the site of the parish church since before the Norman Conquest and a Roman altar was found during excavations in 1847. During the Civil War the town was a Royalist stronghold. The coal industry was the main reason for the town's growth during the Industrial Revolution and remains important today. The major tourist attraction in the town is the new Wigan Pier development beside the Leeds and Liverpool Canal, which was officially opened by Her Majesty the Queen in March 1986. The sight of the Royal Barge sailing through Wigan would have been undreamed of only a few years

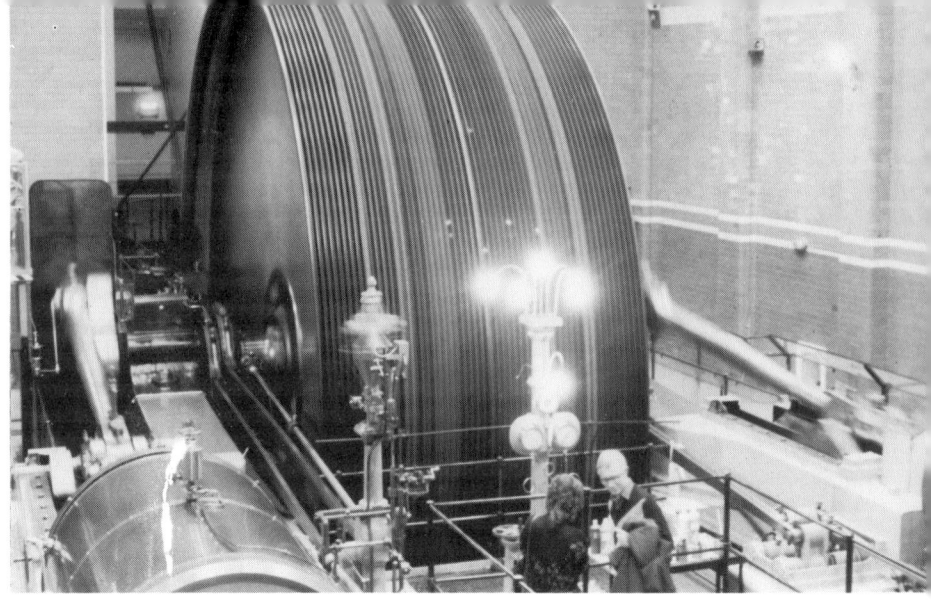

The Mill Engine, Trencherfield Mill, Wigan Pier (*Photo:* Andrew Macfarlane)

before. There are two sites which make up the museum, the Heritage Centre at the pier itself and Trencherfield Mill which are linked by a water-bus service along the canal. The Heritage Centre contains a museum of working life of about 1900 while the Machinery Hall at Trencherfield Mill houses an enormous steam mill engine which has been restored to working order and a demonstration of the entire cotton-producing process takes place at weekends. Another of the attractions is the reconstructed L & Y signal-box from Douglas Bank East on the Wigan–Southport line. Wigan Pier has been a great success in attracting visitors and gained the British Tourist Authority 'Come to Britain' Award in 1986. To reach the museum turn right ouside Wallgate Station and continue walking for ten to fifteen minutes, turning left into Pottery Road shortly before reaching the pier. Frequent buses also run along

The 'actual' pier at Wigan (*Photo:* Andrew Macfarlane)

Wallgate passing North Western Station. The site is open daily throughout the year except Christmas Day from 10 a.m. to 5 p.m.

MANCHESTER VICTORIA – PRESTON VIA CHORLEY
by Andrew Macfarlane and Malcolm Richardson

We begin our journey from Manchester Victoria Station which was opened by the Lancashire & Yorkshire Railway in 1844. Extensive restoration work has been carried out on the station in recent years including the cleaning of the attractive stonework of the front~ge. Worthy of note are the large tiled map of the Lancashire & Yorkshire system and The Dome buffet and bar with its restored interior, both of which are on our left as we enter the station.

Usually, most Preston-bound trains will leave from Platform 13, consisting of various lengths and types of diesel multiple-unit and as a rule work through to Blackpool North. As we depart, to our left are the platforms of the former Manchester Exchange Station, closed in 1969, beyond which can be glimpsed Manchester Cathedral. The train snakes past Irwell Bridge and Deal Street signal boxes on the left, while on the right can be seen Chester's brewery now owned by Whitbreads. We soon arrive at Salford Station. Granada TV studios can be glimpsed to the left. The Liverpool line disappears to our left and we curve round to the right, passing the Hope Street stone terminal on our left which is served by block trains from the Peak District. The approach to Windsor Bridge signal box is now in a transitional period as it will, by 1988, form the Windsor link to Manchester Piccadilly and on the left can be seen the newly constructed platforms at Salford Crescent Station. The line to Wigan via Atherton diverges to our left, and we enter a cutting running parallel with the filled-in Manchester, Bolton and Bury Canal. To our left is the Brindle Heath refuse transfer station of the Greater Manchester Waste Disposal Authority from which trainloads of treated refuse are taken to Appley Bridge beyond Wigan. Agecroft Junction signal box to our left controlled the junction with the spur from Brindle Heath Junction on the Atherton line which was used by Manchester – Blackburn trains which called at Pendleton. The spur was, however, closed in May 1987. We now begin to climb as we pass Agecroft Colliery to our left and Agecroft power station to our right, which are linked to each other by conveyor.

Continuing on, we reach Clifton Station, formerly Clifton Junction, where the former trackbed to Bury, closed in 1966, can be seen to the right. This station was the scene of bitter rivalry between the Lancashire & Yorkshire and the East Lancashire railway companies between 1849 and 1854. In fact, in 1849 a blockade occurred and eventually no less than ten trains became involved in the mess although no one was injured and there was no violence. This station is served by Manchester to Blackburn trains only, and traces of its former importance and illustrious history have all but disappeared. Beyond Clifton we have a good view to our right of the thirteen-arch viaduct which carried the line to Bury over the River Irwell before we pass under the M62 motorway. We enter a wooded cutting and we reach Kearsley Station, formerly known as 'Stoneclough', and also served by Blackburn-bound trains only. Still climbing we enter the left-hand bore of the two Farnworth tunnels, which are 295 yards long. The recent proposal for electrification would have involved coasting through the tunnels to avoid the problem of limited clearance for the overhead wires. The next station is Farnworth, birthplace of England footballer Alan Ball. The Biblical-sounding Moses Gate is next, once used by employees of the nearby Horrockses cotton-mill.

The former line formation to Bury disappears behind Burnden Park, the fine Bolton Wanderers Football Ground, clearly visible on the right. Bolton Station, formerly Bolton Trinity Street, at the time of writing is undergoing reconstruction. New colourlight signalling was commissioned in 1985. Bolton, like many other towns in Lancashire and Yorkshire, owes its development to the textile industry. The damp climate was found to be ideal for spinning yarn and later cotton and the numerous surviving mills in the area are testimony to the past importance of the industry. Today, many are used for other purposes though some still process man-made fibres. Others have been demolished, their chimneys providing work for local steeplejack, Fred Dibnah, who has become something of a celebrity.

Leaving Bolton, the Blackburn line immediately diverges to our right, and we enter the left hand of the two Moor Lane tunnels which date from 1840. Bullfield West signal-box is to our left, and we note the surviving semaphore signalling both here and farther on at Lostock Junction. Its former station is reopening in view of the considerable new housing nearby. The line to Wigan and Southport diverges here to the left. We take the line over Red Moss towards Blackrod. At this high point the former locomotive works at Horwich is visible on the right behind the backcloth of houses and the Railway Mechanics' Institute. Behind is Rivington Pike, whose summit is topped by a tower which is a landmark visible on a clear day from Lytham. Conversely on a clear evening from Rivington Tower one can see Blackpool Tower. We slow for our second stop at Blackrod and the surviving side of the triangular junction with the Horwich branch trails in from the right. Note the L & Y signal-box on our left, the 'fringe' box to Preston power signal-box. Anderton service station on the M61 is visible to our right and beyond is Winter Hill, whose summit is nearly 1,500 feet above sea-level. On a clear day the BBC and ITV transmitters stand out against the sky while burial mounds near the summit are thought to be 3,500 years old.

Two miles beyond Blackrod is Adlington, where you should alight for the beautiful Rivington and Anglezarke areas. Beyond Adlington, the former Wigan–Chorley line joined from the left until its final closure in 1971. Three miles on, we come to Chorley, whose station was recently rebuilt. This bustling market town was once a vital staging post on the main turnpike road, running north and south. Henry Tate, one of the founders of Tate & Lyle sugar-refiners was born in Chorley in 1819. He also built and endowed the Tate Gallery in London. Astley Hall, on the main A6 in the town centre, and open throughout the year is a preserved Elizabethan mansion which contains the bed in which Oliver Cromwell slept after the Battle of Preston in 1648. Chorley is also the home of the soft drink Vimto, whose recipe is still a closely guarded secret. Leaving Chorley, the line drops sharply and dives through a short tunnel into a deep cutting where we pass beneath the unique Flying Arches which span the line. Erected in 1843, the single-course stones at the centre are only 12 inches thick and were constructed to hold back, with the assistance of retaining walls, the sides of a cutting driven through difficult clay soil, which it proved impossible to tunnel through. The construction proved to be so good, they have since required only minimal maintenance. To our right we soon see the Royal Ordnance factory. We pass the deserted platforms of the former Chorley Royal Ordnance Station which still looks very much as it must have done when thousands of munitions workers detrained there during the Second World War.

Our line now becomes single line for a short distance before we join the West Coast main line at Euxton Junction. We pass under the M6 and arrive at the four-platformed Leyland Station. Just a few hundred yards from the station is the British Commercial Vehicle Museum with a wide range of exhibits dating from 1896 to the present day. Leaving Leyland, the Leyland truck plant is on the left, adjacent to the site of Farington Station, closed in 1960. We pass under the line to East Lancashire, then the lines from there and Ormskirk merge with ours at Farington Curve Junction. We then cross over the former trackbed to Southport, closed in 1964. Before our train crosses the River Ribble, the old railway bridge that carried the East Lancashire line into Preston Station can be clearly seen on the right. Also on the right, just before entering the station, we pass the former Park Hotel, which opened in 1882, two years after the new Preston Station. The train then arrives in Preston Station, hub of the Lancashire rail network, and 31 miles from Manchester.

BOLTON–WIGAN
by Andrew Macfarlane

The service from Bolton to Wigan Wallgate is basically hourly and many of the trains run through to either Southport or Kirkby. The line was until 1922 part of the Lancashire & Yorkshire Railway. We take the Preston line out of Bolton, diverging to the left at Lostock Junction. We run through open country and pass under the M61 motorway. The Metal Box factory visible to our left is rail-connected and we arrive at Westhoughton Station, which has bus-stop shelters. After Westhoughton we cross over the former Dobbs Brow cut-off line and join the line from Manchester via Atherton at Crow Nest Junction. We call at Hindley and Ince before arriving at Wigan Wallgate, 9½ miles from Bolton.

BLACKBURN–BOLTON
by Tim Young

The cotton-mill towns of East Lancashire wanted a convenient means of getting their products to Manchester and with the advent of railways a line across the moors to Bolton was built with this primary aim. Virtually all the mills have long since closed, yet the line remains open mainly for passengers and is one of the unrecognised gems of the North West rail network. The train leaves Blackburn and heads towards Preston passing sidings on its left before turning south at Bolton Junction, climbing and curving away towards its first stop at Darwen. On the way to Darwen, Ewood Park, home of Blackburn Rovers can be clearly seen on the right while on the hilltop in the distance is Darwen Tower, erected in 1897 to celebrate the Diamond Jubilee of Queen Victoria's reign. It makes a very pleasant walk from Darwen Station. Within ten minutes of Darwen Station, there are landscaped gardens on the slopes of Darwen Moor at Bold Venture Park, while ¾ mile away Sunnyhurst Woods are also worth a visit. After the somewhat spartan station at Darwen the train continues climbing into open country before going through Sough Tunnel, the longest tunnel in Lancashire. The train re-emerges into the daylight, still climbing, and with the scenery getting ever more spectacular. The line flattens out at Sough summit, and the view is especially good over the moors to the left as we come to Entwistle. This isolated little station, high up on the moors is an excellent base for walkers. After Entwistle the train passes Wayoh Reservoir on the left before passing under turreted bridges near Turton Tower. This rectangular stone building, dating from about 1400, can be reached by alighting at the next station at Bromley Cross, from which one can either walk or catch a bus. Shortly before arrival at Bromley Cross though, the train passes Jumbles Reservoir on the left, surrounded by the Jumbles Country Park. About ten minutes' walk from the station, this park offers a variety of walks, with fishing, and other recreations. The picturesque Last Drop village is also near by with olde-worlde buildings. The line now starts to descend off the moors and, as the northern outskirts of Bolton are reached, so Hall i' th' Wood Station, opened in 1986 and already the target of local vandals. It takes its somewhat strange name from a building of the same name about ten minutes' walk away that was the home of Samuel Crompton from 1758 to 1782. Preserved and furnished in the Jacobean period, it was here that Crompton built his first spinning mule. The floodlights of Burnden Park on our left tell us we have not far to go, and after passing through a short tunnel we bend sharply left into the large and imposing Bolton Station. Bolton itself is worthy of a visit with its good shopping centre, or you can carry on on the same train to Manchester or change at Bolton for trains to either Preston and Blackpool or Wigan and Southport.

MANCHESTER VICTORIA – BURY
by Felix Schmid

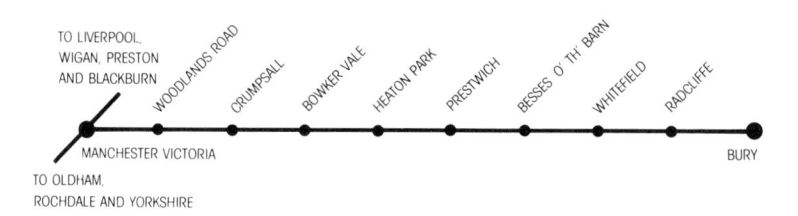

The first railway line reached Bury in 1846, built by the Manchester, Bury, & Rossendale Railway as a branch from the Manchester & Bolton Railway. Its double-track line left the route of the present Manchester to Bolton main line at Clifton Junction, crossing the River Irwell on a massive stone viaduct which exists to this day. The tracks reached the present line to Bury at a point just north of Radcliffe and, the alignment of this early line stands out clearly in the countryside. In 1845 the company was integrated into the East Lancashire Railway, a name adopted by the group who are in the process of reopening the line from Bury to Rawtenstall.

The journey to Bury starts, at the time of writing, in one of the terminal bays of Victoria Station. Since 1916 the line has been electrified using the third-rail system – unfortunately it all needs replacing. As the Bury line is part of the Light Rail scheme for Manchester, all this may soon change. We leave the train shed towards the east, on our right a remarkable commercial building with a richly decorated frontage towards the road while the side facing the railway is a simple brick wall.

Our train parallels the main lines to Leeds for a few hundred yards before it disappears into a tunnel turning north. On leaving the tunnel the line bridges the River Irk and the Cheetham Hill Loop Line. Past Queens Road Junction Box we reach Woodlands Road Halt and continue to Crumpsall Station, a reasonable structure with a well-proportioned overbridge. The brick road bridge near the station over a deep cutting represents a minor engineering truimph. Crumpsall is close to the North Manchester General Hospital.

After an initial stretch of inner-city waste land we are now firmly in the suburbs. The journey is consequently quite uneventful. Before we reach Bowker Vale Station, though, there are some small reservoirs on the right while Heaton Park and, on a hill, Heaton Hall form a dramatic backdrop. Like most of the stations on this line the one at Bowker has been extensively refurbished and similarly vandalised. A tunnel allows the Bury line to traverse the park without disturbing the peace and quiet and enjoyment of thousands of visitors during summer. Heaton Park Station, a short distance from the end of the tunnel, is followed by a stop at Prestwich which serves a comfortable suburb and the mental hospital.

After hurtling across both Bury Old Road and the M62 motorway and stopping at Besses o' th' Barn, we continue on to Whitefield where the train enters a short tunnel and then a deep cutting. We leave this rather restricting environment to traverse the River Irwell on a viaduct. To the right opens a pleasant vale, in the foreground a mill building. The train soon stops at Radcliffe where we look out on to a landscape which looks like the true 'cliché of t'old North'—Gracie Fields' land. On the left back to back terraces and a Neo-Gothic church. In the good old days there was a spur from Radcliffe Station to the line linking Bolton and Bury Knowsley Street, which closed in 1970. The location where the old line from Clifton Junction joined our route is no longer evident but a reconstruction is easy using the appropriate Ordnance Survey map.

On the left now open country offers fine views towards Winter Hill and Belmont as well as affording a look back into transport history, for we are travelling along a section of the disused Manchester, Bolton and Bury Canal, infamous for its water-supply problems. Elton Reservoir is on the left as we clear the River Irwell and approach the junction between the metals of the preserved East Lancashire Railway and double track leading to the new Bury Interchange Station. On the right, shortly before reaching the island platform in a deep cutting, you may catch a glimpse of the buffer stop of the freight-only line to Rochdale via Heywood.

Bury Interchange is new, huge, and depends entirely on a well-functioning bus system which serves a very substantial hinterland reaching out as far as Haslingden and Rawtenstall. Bury itself is a small town with a clear centre, but reaching out into the district as if equipped with tentacles. Bury has a good market and an unexciting Town Hall, but it boasts at least two extravagant monuments to civic pride in Manchester Road—both St Mary's Catholic Church and the Public Library are adorned by rich stone-carvings, not necessarily perfect, but very pleasing.

Bury's previous main station, Bolton Street, is now owned by the East Lancashire Railway Preservation Society.

A WALK ROUND HEATON PARK
By Felix Schmid

From Heaton Park Station cross the A665 and enter the park. Turn left up the hill, past a copse and meadows where you may meet with a herd of Angus cattle—if you are lucky, there will even be some calves! Veer to the right leaving farm buildings on the left and head for the Japanese Pond down in a little vale, complete with wooden temple and stepping-stones. Follow the narrow path ascending through an open wood and enjoy a view over part of the park before walking down towards one of the main metalled avenues. Turn left to reach the rose-garden and exhibition farm. The stables house a representative selection of farm animals and their young as well as a collection of antique farm machinery. Just across the way from the display farm is Heaton Hall, a vast, grey mansion built in 1772 by James Wyatt. It is famed for its plasterwork frescoes, paintings, and sculptures. The park, Central and East Manchester form the panorama from the geometrical garden in front of the hall. Beyond the hall, turn left before the golf-course and head for the folly and the commanding all-round view.

Return to the avenue between stables and hall and wander downhill to the boating-lake, with its refreshment room. Follow, on foot, the quaint signs prescribing the direction of navigation and you will reach the lakeside terminus of the Heaton Park Tramway. On a summer week-end you might catch one of the restored Manchester trams for the ride through the woods and along one of the avenues to the East Gate.

The double-track section was originally used by Manchester Corporation Tramways to take day trippers to the park. Leave the park and turn right on to the A576, on the other side the River Irk, and follow this road for about ½ mile as far as the railway overbridge where you turn right again to reach Bowker Vale Station. Total distance approximately 3 miles – about two hours including some sightseeing.

AROUND ROCHDALE
By Felix Sxhmid

Several bus services link Bury Interchange with Rochdale town centre and Bus Station. The more interesting route follows the B6222 above the River Roch and close to open country, via Hooley Bridge. In Rochdale the buses pass the Public Library on the left and the Town Hall on the right. The latter building may look familiar to a Mancunian: indeed, it is modelled on Manchester's Town Hall and is proof of the rivalry between the burghers of the two towns which were similar in size in the early nineteenth century. Rochdale was and still is an important manufacturing centre, although the textile sector no longer boasts a hundred factories as in the 1930s. The town was the birthplace of the retail co-operative movement; the Rochdale Pioneers opened their first shop in Toad Lane in 1844, it is now a museum to the movement.

Rochdale is on the edge of good walking country, the moors are less than 3 miles from the centre and the Pennine Way is 6 miles away. Hollingworth Lake offers excellent sailing and large reservoirs are dotted about the landscape. A two-hour walk from the centre of Rochdale, via Spotland Bridge, Catley Lane Head, and Rooley Moor, above Whitworth, brings you to the top of Cowpe Moss which, at 1,560 feet, on a good day, gives the best all-round view in the North West. From Cowpe Moss another two-hour walk leads to Edenfield and Stubbins Station.

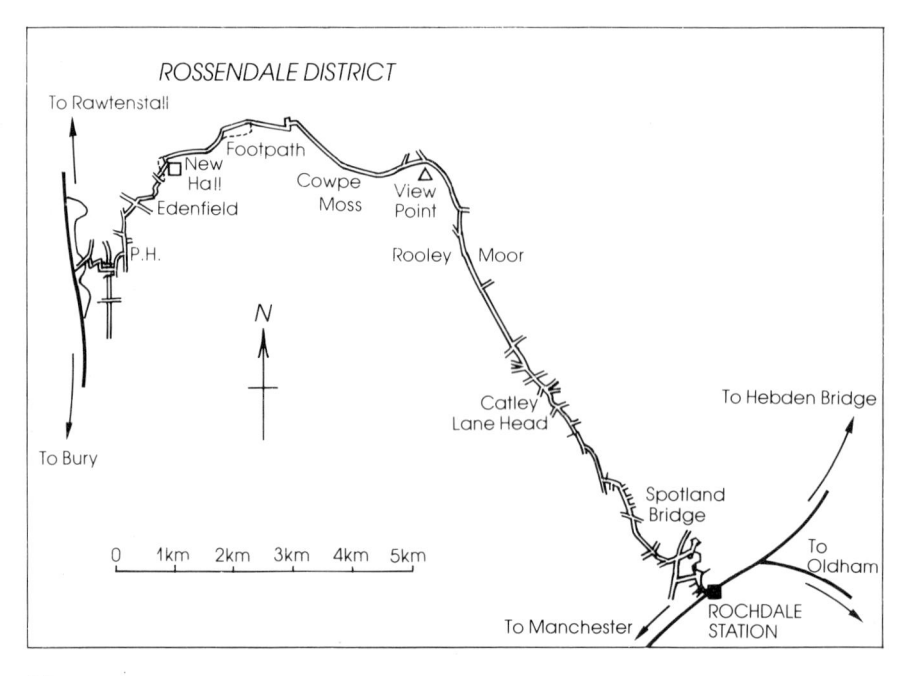

HEBDEN BRIDGE – ROSE GROVE AND MANCHESTER VICTORIA

by Tim Young

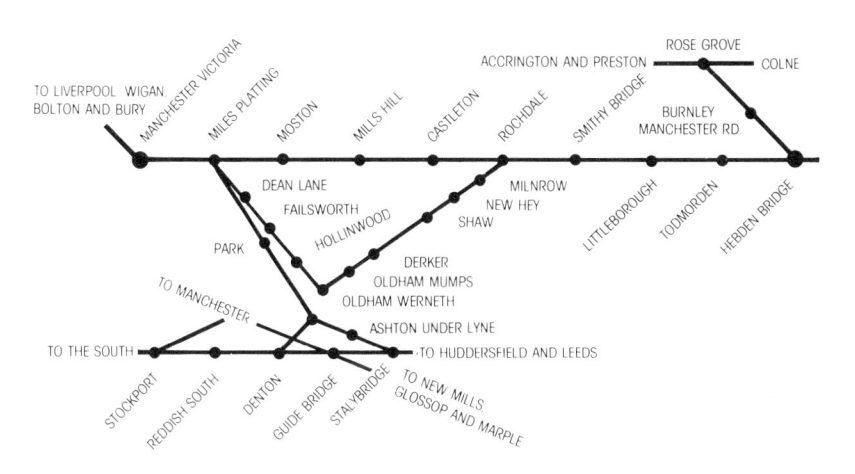

Hebden Bridge is a charming little town set in the heart of the Pennines and, as such, is an excellent centre for those wanting to walk or cycle in the surrounding hills. For those less energetic, a stroll down its main street or along the canal towpath can be equally rewarding, The station, on the Caldervale line, is also worthy of note. Built of stone, it still retains many features that would have been commonplace in years gone by. The most obvious are the various signs, seen at most stations, for such facilities as waiting-rooms, toilets, and exits, which at Hebden Bridge are made of dark brown wood with the lettering embossed and painted white. British Rail are to be complimented as the station nameplates, normally black lettering on a white background, are white lettering on a light brown background which tone in excellently with the Victorian atmosphere of the station.

Our train will be coming out from Leeds and after departure from Hebden Bridge passes through a succession of four tunnels. The first is Weasel Hall Tunnel and soon after emerging into the daylight again, we move from the Eastern to the London Midland Region, as the train passes through a tree-lined valley before the next three tunnels, which are Horsefall, Castle Hill, and Millwood in that order. Stoodley Pike can be seen on the hilltop to our left as we come to a parting of the ways at Hall Royd Junction.

Until 1984, the lines going away to the right were only used for freight trains and special excursion trains to Blackpool for the summer and the illuminations. In the spring of 1984, the National & Provincial Building Society, formed the previous year by the merger of the Bradford-based Provincial Building Society with the Burnley Building Society, subsidised the introduction of a regular service for the first time in several years in order to facilitate the movement of their staff between Burnley and Bradford, One train ran leaving Preston about 7.30 a.m. running to Bradford only, calling at principal intermediate stations and returning to Preston in the early evening. Although the cost of running this service was being met by the building society, any member of the public could also use it. In October 1984, British Rail launched its own regular service of about half a dozen trains a day, all of which were

55

extended to Leeds at the Yorkshire end and one or two extended to Blackpool at the Lancashire end, the remainder terminating at Preston, under the brand-name of 'The Roses link'.

After turning right, the train goes through Kitson Wood Tunnel, then follows the valley as it skirts round the edge of Todmorden. Soon we are climbing to Copy Pit summit (749 feet) before entering Holme Tunnel. In February 1986 a trackman making a routine examination of the line discovered a deformity in the tunnel wall, and the line was immediately closed while it was investigated. In fact the whole hill through which the tunnel passed was moving and it took seven months for engineers to repair the tunnel and install reinforcing 'ribs', so you will note that the train you are on has bars across the windows and slows right down as it enters the tunnel. The 'ribs' can be clearly seen at the Yorkshire end. We emerge into open country with good views especially to the right, before going through the curved Towneley Tunnel and passing Towneley crossing, the only signal box on the line. You get a good panoramic view of Burnley to the right before coming to Burnley Manchester Road Station. This station was opened in September 1986 near to the site of a previous station of the same name closed in November 1961. One unusual feature is that it opened with a bus service as its opening was scheduled to coincide with the reopening of the line after its enforced closure due to earth movement at Holme Tunnel. As previously mentioned though, the reopening was delayed for two weeks while further work was done on the track through Holme tunnel and bars fitted to train windows. The station, though, was opened on time with services provided by the bus that had run for seven months between Rose Grove and Hebden Bridge in lieu of the trains. Then the train rattles across Gannow Junction and through Rose Grove Station, where all trains to and from Leeds used to stop until Burnley Manchester Road was opened. Now your train will carry on apace until its next scheduled stop at Accrington.

If you are travelling from Hebden Bridge to Manchester Victoria, you will take the line to the left at Hall Royd Junction. In common with a lot of towns in the area, the railway enters Todmorden on a high viaduct at rooftop-level. The station, like others, is built of stone, and there is an attractive Rampant Lion stone plaque on the Leeds-bound platform. After Todmorden the train goes through the curiously named Winterbutlee Tunnel and soon after enters the 1¾-mile-long Summit Tunnel which was the scene of a spectacular derailment in 1984 when a train of oil tankers left the lines and caught fire. Many local residents had to be temporarily evacuated as flames shot many feet into the air from its several ventilation shafts. As you pass through the tunnel, you also pass into Lancashire and emerge into daylight to run through Littleborough Station and Smithy Bridge, another new station to be opened as a nearby tunnel was reopened. As with Burnley Manchester Road, there was a previous Smithy Bridge closed in 1960. By now the terrain has changed dramatically from the majestic hills of the Pennines to the flatter industrial plain as the line from Oldham curves in from the left as we enter Rochdale. Rochdale is best known as being the birthplace of the 'Co-op' and of Gracie Fields. Its best-known present-day celebrity is the rotund Liberal MP, Cyril Smith, whose constituency it is. Castleton, Mills Hill, and Moston soon follow before Newton Heath depot comes up on our left. We are now well within the boundary of Greater Manchester and at the next station, Miles Platting, V-shaped and built round the junction, we join up with the Diggle route from Leeds for the final few minutes before arriving at Manchester's Victoria Station.

ROCHDALE–MANCHESTER VICTORIA VIA OLDHAM
by Felix Schmid

Rochdale Station is situated above the town centre, on stone and brick arches. The station buildings are pleasantly modern and adequate for the good train service of the town. The local train for the Oldham line waits either at the northern bay platform or on the through road from Manchester—many services travel the full loop. The Oldham line's single track runs, at first, parallel to the main line for Hebden Bridge and Halifax. The track then swings right, past the Rugby Ground at Newbold, and bridges the Rochdale Canal. This canal was built to link Manchester to the industrial towns of the Calder Valley and to provide a cheap route to Leeds via the Calder and Hebble Navigation. It is being reopened in stages after the last commercial through traffic ceased in the 1930s.

Through open country and a cutting we reach Milnrow halt of which only the northern platform is still in use. Butterworth Mill on the left obscures the view to the

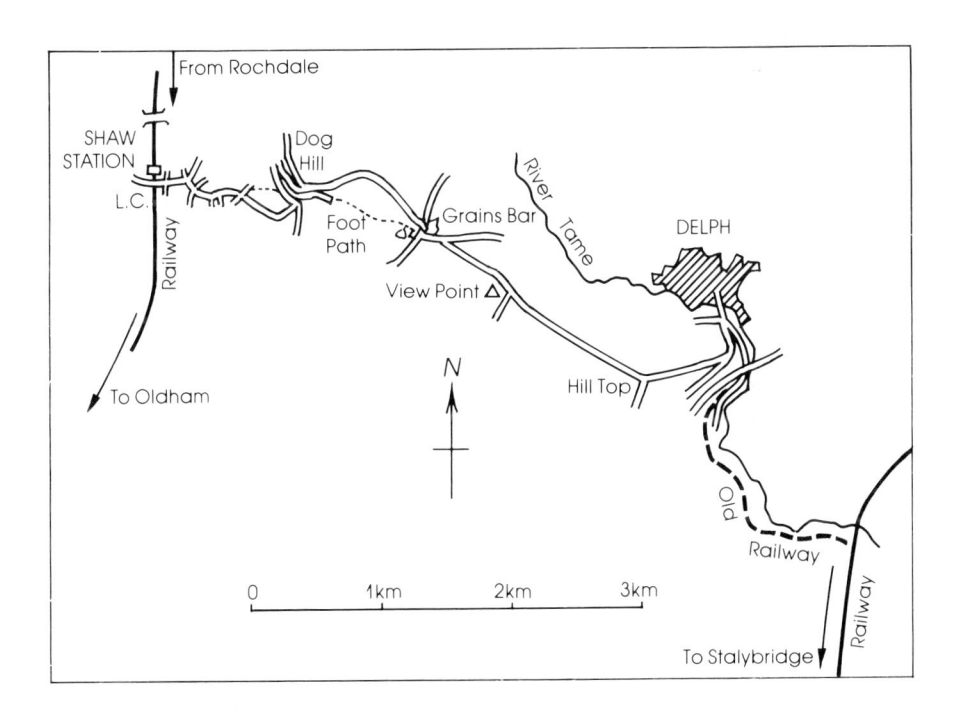

hills round Denshaw–Bleakedgate Moor and White Hill. It is worth noting that the vast majority of older houses is built from stone rather than bricks. Building materials from the local quarries were, of course, much cheaper than bricks from the Potteries.

We pass under the M62 motorway, enter a deep cutting, and pause at New Hey Station, once an important goods transfer point with a Lancashire and Yorkshire Railway cotton warehouse, now part of a factory. Still going uphill we follow the River Beal and the A663. The open vale with good views to left and right turns into a wooded

A Pacer unit between Shaw and Derker on 22 February 1986 (*Photo:* Tom Heavyside)

clough and we come out into what is, on the left, a bleak and rugged landscape. With the huge Rutland Mill on the left we regain double track and stop at Shaw Station. A one-hour walk would take us from here eastwards to the quaint village of Delph in the Upper Tame Valley. From there we could use the trackbed of the old railway to reach Uppermill.

With Dawn Mill on the right we leave Shaw Station for some real countryside. We are surrounded by hill farms, alas for only about a mile's journey. Fields become rubble strewn and an old factory appears on the right as we pass through Royton Junction Station, closed like the branch line which served the industrial community of Royton. With on the right modern estates and on the left traditional terraces we arrive at wood-built Derker Halt, one of the new Greater Manchester Council sponsored stations. Through a cutting and between bleak and crumbling factory buildings we arrive at Oldham Mumps, a well-kept station serving all of Oldham now that Central Station no longer exists. On the left is a large open space, formerly occupied by the important freight sidings. Towards the east one can just about make out traces of the old line to Greenfield and Huddersfield.

On the left, as we continue towards Manchester, are the remains of the dismantled link to Ashton-under-Lyne. The train rapidly gathers momentum running downhill through two tunnels; almost reluctantly we stop at Oldham Werneth, a much-vandalised halt. Many years ago we could have carried on straight ahead to Middleton Junction, but the link has been severed. Turning south instead we travel on an embankment with, on the left, traditional back-to-back housing. This stretch of our journey is best enjoyed in the evening with a glorious sunset over Manchester and Chadderton Mill on the right reflected in its pond. Houses and mills as far as one can see, it is almost like the olden days.

Hollinwood Station is followed by a quarry on the right and, joining from the north, the Rochdale Canal and its towpath. With Moston Brook and its peculiarly unnatural valley on the right we call at Failsworth, a vandalised vandal-proof shelter. Descending past the giant GMC waste transfer depot, again on the right, we enter a cutting and stop at Dean Lane Halt. Onwards we roll past the motive power depot at Newton Heath where we join the Manchester—Rochdale main line which carries our train to Miles Platting Station and hence, together with the line from Stalybridge, to Manchester Victoria.

STALYBRIDGE – MANCHESTER VICTORIA
by Felix Schmid

After a refreshing drink, and perhaps a sandwich, in the station's own public house we leave Stalybridge on board either one of the Leeds to Liverpool expresses or a local train. The railway from Stalybridge to Leeds via Marsden, Huddersfield, and Dewsbury was built by the LNWR in 1849 to compete with the Lancashire & Yorkshire Railway through Rochdale and the Calder Valley, and also to tap the increasingly important towns *en route* which were up to then served by totally inadequate canals, navigable only by the narrowest of narrow boats. From Stalybridge to Manchester the LNWR had running powers over the L&Y.

The new industrial units on the right take up the space where once there used to be sidings and the terminal bays for the local trains. A few hundred yards farther on, the main line turns north, away from the chord line to Guide Bridge and thence, to Stockport. In a deep cutting, crossed by many road bridges, and through a short tunnel we reach Ashton-under-Lyne Station. Only few vestiges of its heyday remain, apart from some stairways built from glazed white bricks. The bus station is only a short distance away from the railway station and offers a number of services out into the countryside.

While passing underneath the A627 we can just about detect, on the right, traces of the former Great Central branch line to Oldham. Ashton Moss North Junction, named after a large expanse of fields still used agriculturally, appears on our left. Trains from the North use the western leg of the junction triangle to reach Sheffield from Manchester Victoria. Immediately after passing a disused trackbed the train enters a cutting crossed by a footbridge which many years ago must have carried the Hollinwood branch of the Ashton Canal. The Manchester district of Droylsden is on our left.

With the end of the cutting we have entered the valley of the River Medlock or 'Medlock Vale', as it rightly deserves to be called. The countryside along the River Medlock has been transformed! Where dereliction once ruled the land, we now see newly planted copses, poisonous tips have been replaced by rolling hills, and a green oasis is forming in the city. Only a few more years and the wanderer on the tracks and footpaths criss-crossing the vale will no longer realise that this area used to be one of the most polluted dumps in the country.

The River Medlock is crossed in picturesque surroundings; the nice views are on the left, that is unless you are interested in 1960s tower blocks. The embankment of a disused industrial branch is still visible even though it has been integrated into the urban renewal project. Again on our left an unusual sight: a complete and seemingly well-maintained cattle-unloading station, part of Manchester Abattoirs, waits for traffic which British Rail has been unable to carry for many years. Park Station serves the abattoir and a dwindling number of factories in the area, of which Mather & Platt's Park works is the most prominent architecturally (on the right). Immediately after the halt is the triangular junction of the goods railway to Beswick and Ashburys, which was once part of a direct link between the then London Road and Victoria stations.

We cross the Rochdale Canal and join the line from Leeds via Rochdale and Halifax at Miles Platting Junction Station, a curious, reasonably well-preserved group of structures amid crumbling factories. The dismantled flyover after the station took the trains into Oldham Road goods yard, whose buildings disappeared at the beginning of the 1980s. From here to Victoria Station the train trundles through a waste land of torn-up sidings and wide open spaces. On the right is the valley of the River Irk, a desolate, depressing sight – a reminder of the devastating influence of rapid industrialisation on the environment. On the other side of the valley are the main carriage sidings, well guarded by the huge tower of Strangeways Prison – a monument to Victorian efforts aimed at improving the standards of correctional institutions. The River Irk disappears under the railway line as we bank down into the station, stopping at Platform 11.

Manchester Victoria

Victoria Station was opened in 1844 as a joint venture of the Liverpool & Manchester and Lancashire & Yorkshire railway companies. Parts of the station are built over the River Irk which joins the Irwell at the bottom of Hunts Bank Approach. The main building, overlooking the station approach, dates from the early 1900s. The green space in front of this attractive and imposing edifice was occupied, until the 1980s, by the former general offices of the L & Y. Victoria Station has a few features which are worth noting.

Platform 11, mentioned above, is deemed to be Europe's longest platform at 2,194 feet. It was extended to its full length in 1884 when the LNWR built Exchange Station, now demolished. The platform is no longer used over its full length but it has not been removed. Even some of the old canopy survives. The central sections of the through roads 12 to 16 are covered by a single-span roof, the terminating tracks are protected from the elements by a multi-span structure, part of which is missing. In the latter area there is space for the introduction of the Manchester Light Rail system.

The wall to the right of the old-fashioned wood-panelled booking office is decorated with a map of the Lancashire & Yorkshire Railway, exactly reproduced on ceramic wall tiles. Immediately behind the map is the refreshment room which has recently been restored to its full splendour. The eating area has a domed glass roof with golden decorations, attractive from both outside and inside! It is an excellent example of Art Deco design. The furniture is, unfortunately, somewhat too modern. Having partaken of ambrosia or nectar do not overlook the well-designed bookstall before rushing for your connection.

STOCKPORT – STALYBRIDGE
by Felix Schmid

Stockport Station forms the southern borderpost to the area covered by this rail guide. To the visitor from the North, the railway lines radiating from Stockport open up the Cheshire Plains, Derbyshire, and the Potteries. Stockport is the first stop on the main railway line from Manchester Piccadilly to London Euston. All the trains from Manchester to Shrewsbury and the South West, Birmingham, London, and Buxton stop at this hub of the North West's rail system. Descriptions of most lines from Stockport will be found in the companion volume to this publication, *Cheshire and North Wales by Rail*.

The two-car multiple-unit waiting on Platform 3A is overlooked by most passengers on the expresses from the South. This train, though, on the last remaining terminal platform at Stockport, is important, it is even part of the InterCity network. It links the main line from Euston to the Trans-Pennine services from Liverpool and Manchester Victoria to Leeds and York. The short line also carries a train with almost romantic overtones – the late-night York to Shrewsbury mail via Stockport and Crewe. This train includes a single passenger coach – a slow train – ideal for delayed travellers!

The train lumbers across Stockport Viaduct, and across the giant bus station, the River Mersey, and the M63 motorway. A few traces remain of the former goods railway line from Woodley to Timperley, most notable the cutting and tunnel in the red rock overlooking Mersey Square. The train leaves the main London – Manchester line at Heaton Norris Junction, just after the LNWR goods warehouse on the right. After passing under Stockport Road we catch a glimpse of an attractive public house on the right – The Ash Hotel – all glazed brick and etched glass. Through patches of allotments and decaying industrial backyards, one of which houses a freight-wagon leasing company, we reach the island platform of Reddish South, a small primitive structure. The industrial archaeologist, of course, would have been looking out for the course of the Stockport Canal which crosses the railway line a few hundred yards before this station (see *A Canal Wall*).

Soon the valley of the River Tame opens to our right with, behind it, the 'foothills' round Charlesworth of the Derbyshire Peak District. In the foreground are the meandering river, reservoirs, and the many-arched viaduct of the Manchester – Marple line. We cross this line and travel, on an embankment, through fields as far as the M67 motorway, in whose shadow the train stops at the dilapidated halt for Denton. Behind the dam on the left is Audenshaw Reservoir, Manchester's biggest. After a few hundred yards we reach Denton Junction where a double-track railway line forks off to the left. This provides a link to the line from Ashton-under-Lyne to Manchester – at Ashton Moss North Junction. Trains from Blackpool and the North use this line to reach Stockport from Manchester Victoria. These trains then travel via Hazel Grove to Sheffield or Nottingham.

A short distance beyond the junction our line changes to single track and joins, in front of a well-proportioned church and spire, the old main line from Manchester to the Woodhead Pass. We enter Guide Bridge Station and stop just long enough to have a look at the well-kept station buildings and the platforms. With the removal of the d.c. electrified freight lines to the east, Guide Bridge and its once-large sidings and traction depot have lost their importance. Immediately after the station we swing off to the left, past sidings and Hawke works, an important manufacturer of electrical equipment. Dukinfield is on the right.

On the left appears the Ashton Canal, there are no cargo boats left, but ever-more pleasure-craft use this section of the Cheshire Ring. Ashton-under-Lyne is on our left as we cross the River Tame. The Peak Forest Canal approaches from the right, fords the River Tame on an aqueduct, and joins the Ashton Canal on our left.

We cross the Ashton Canal just before it becomes the Huddersfield Narrow Canal (disused and blocked by concrete lock-'gates'), with on our left the very substantial church which dominates Ashton. We are now travelling east in a cutting with a backdrop of moorland hills, the view to the right being obscured by a huge mill. The tracks joining from the left carry trains to Manchester. We continue past the junction on to the hillside embankment – this is Stalybridge Station from whose platform we get a good view of the hills and a small mill with a characteristic octagonal stack.

The main station building is attractive albeit on a much-reduced scale compared to its heyday. The station has a great asset though: a refreshment room-cum-station pub, walls covered with old railway photographs, serving the usual beverages, and also delights like chilli butties! The twenty minutes of waiting for the connection to Manchester can be pleasant in such surroundings.

THE BLACKPOOL TRAMWAY
by Malcolm Richardson

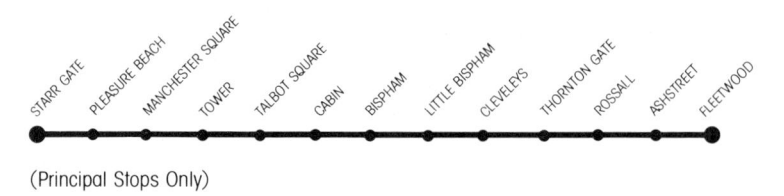

(Principal Stops Only)

In 1985 the Blackpool Tramway celebrated its centenary with several vintage trams and buses being specially brought into Blackpool and Fleetwood for the occasion which proved a great success. In 1986 Fleetwood celebrated its 150 years with a transport cavalcade in Lord Street, the last main town street to contain tram rails outside Blackpool itself.

The railborne traveller's first encounter with trams will usually take place at one of three locations. Alighting at Squires Gate Station turn left at the exit from the station and a short walk down Squires Gate Lane brings Starr Gate where trams start from a terminal loop line through all the way to Fleewood if you so desire.

As an alternative by alighting at Blackpool South Station turn left at Waterloo Road Bridge then a short walk through the shopping area brings you on to the promenade. Look for the South Pier and a tram journey can start here.

Most people arriving at Blackpool North Station would find walking down Talbot Road to the North Pier the best way to catch a tram.

History
The 11-mile course of the tramway along the Fylde coast has an involved history and was the result of amalgamation of the 1898 Blackpool & Fleetwood Tramway Company whose headquarters were at Bispham depot, and the Corporation tramways. The line did not become a through route until 1920 under the Corporation and it was a further ten years before a regular service operated all the way from the promenade to Fleetwood. A private enterprise firm operated from Cocker Street to South Pier from 1885 and sold out to the Corporation in 1892. The Corporation then converted from a troublesome underground conduit system to overhead wires and extended the system at both ends until with the 1926 extension of the line from the Pleasure Beach to Starr Gate it assumed its present proportions.

The coastal route, however, was part of a much more extensive system and between 1896 and 1937 covered inland to Layton, Squires Gate, and Marton as well as the Gynn Square to North Station and through to Lytham from Squires Gate. One by one the routes closed down starting with the Central line in 1936. Next came Lytham Road in 1961 followed by the Marton route in 1962 and then, lastly, in 1963 the Dickson Road route leaving the present coastal route from Starr Gate to Fleetwood as England's last.

The Journey—Starr Gate to Fleetwood
We will assume the traveller boards the tram at Starr Gate, the southern terminus of the line. A frequency of approximately twelve minutes operates in the summer using twelve double-decker trams with eight one-man operated (OMO) trams on the Promenade to Little Bispham section with a twenty-minute service in the winter using the eight OMO cars. This is augmented by extra services during the illuminations.

Leaving Starr Gate on 'open' track which soon changes to 'paved-in' track we pass on the right rows of 1930s-built hotels until reaching Harrowside. Alight here for the Solarium Gardens and putting-green. Passing further 1930s-built hotels including several well-known ones such as the Headlands and the Warwick we soon reach Blackpool's latest attraction, the Sandcastle all-weather indoor entertainment centre which stands on the site of the old South Shore baths. On the right is the most-visited place of entertainment in Blackpool, the Pleasure Beach. There is a loop and turning circle for trams at this location. The next place of interest on the left is South Pier at Station Road. The tram route to Lytham Road terminated opposite here until 1961. Continuing on we reach Waterloo Road. Alight here for Blackpool South Station.

The next major tram stop is Manchester Square opposite the Manchester Hotel, one of Blackpool's busiest in summer. The lines from Rigby Road depot trail in from the right here. Soon we reach Central Pier on the left and on the right can be seen the town's most famous landmark, the Tower. People never lose their fascination for this well-loved structure and rightly so. This stop would have been near to another of Blackpool's well-known landmarks, Central Station, but this closed in 1964 and the Queens Theatre was also demolished. Even Woolworth's store is no more though still standing on your right is Lewis's store covering the site of the Palace Ballroom, demolished in 1960. On the left a little farther on is the North Pier being pleasingly restored in Edwardian style. Again alight here for North Station. At Talbot Square there is a passing loop for trams before entering the hazardous street section of track at the rear of the Metropole Hotel. Moving on to the Queens Promenade section past many hotels we eventually reach Gynn Square which was once an important junction for the trams with the 'backroad' to North Station as it was known to tram crews until closure in 1963.

Onwards past Uncle Tom's Cabin on the right and past the imposing and impressive Miners' Convalescent Home we reach Bispham tram station opposite Red Bank Road. The line to Bispham tram depot, which closed in 1966, trailed off here. It was the headquarters of the 'other firm', as it was known to the Corporation employees because of its Company origins. Next stop is Norbreck Station opposite the Norbreck Castle Hotel. We press on to Little Bispham Station on open sleeper track and gradually move inland from Queens Promenade to Anchorsholme crossing where special traffic lights control the tram crossing. We are soon in Cleveleys shopping area at Victoria Square.

Onwards to Thornton Gate where the permanent way sidings are located; these were once coal sidings. After leaving this location the tram now heads for Rossall and the only 'rural' part of the route. Passing firstly Broadwater and then Copse Road, itself a site of a former depot closed in 1963, we are now entering the very heart of Fleetwood at Ash Street and Lord Street before reaching the terminal line loop at Fleetwood Ferry where one can either board the *Funboat* to the Isle of Man or sample the delights of Fleetwood. The completed journey by tram, a unique experience in Britain today, will have been of an hour's duration from Starr Gate.

THE EAST LANCASHIRE RAILWAY
by Felix Schmid

The East Lancashire Railway's tracks leave BR's Bury line about 1 km from its terminus on an embankment. This is in fact the original route into Bury. The line crosses the trackbed of the old Liverpool–Leeds Railway, last used for a goods service only. The island platform of Bury Bolton Street Station is situated in a cutting a short distance beyond the flyover of Bury Western bypass. The station building at road-level is a 1950s structure, simple but attractive in its own way; the original headquarters of the ELR had been to the east of the railway, on the site now used as a car park. The line disappears under Bolton Street and is joined by the tracks from the depot fan at the point where it emerges from the short tunnel.

Bury Transport Museum has been developed on this former ELR site at Castlecroft. It accommodates a large transport collection and workshops. Exhibits range from the last surviving Ribble Express bus (specially built for the Blackpool−London run) to a Black Five rescued from Barry Yard. There are more than fifteen steam and diesel engines, the majority of which are ex-BR main-line locomotives, a 'Western' for instance. Restoration tasks which would seem superhuman to the uninitiated are tackled as though completion was only months and not years away. Such belief in ultimate success has brought about the reopening of the 4 miles of single-track line to Ramsbottom, with the help of the defunct Greater Manchester Council, Rossendale Council and the Manpower Services Commission.

From the depot connection the ELR continues underneath the northern ring road and follows the eastern valley slope to Fernhill, on the left the viaduct of the former branch to Holcombe Brook, across the River Irwell. On the left a well-preserved mill and, on the right, the northern outskirts of Bury. We cross and recross the Irwell, enter Touchy Hill cutting, and again follow the Irwell on open fields. By now we are well within the country park which is the main reason for the preserved railway's prosperity.

The next stop, Summerseat, in a bend of the river, is placed to give access to the industrial village of Brooksbottom and the river valley, unfortunately blighted over a distance of ½ mile by the M66 motorway. On the right, above the halt, is a once-famous Wesleyan chapel, Rowlands. Our train crosses the Irwell on Brooksbottom Viaduct and enters the tunnel of the same name. Nuttall Tunnel follows, built to pander to the whims of a local squire, whose caricature hewn in stone now adorns the north portal. Nuttall Hall is on the left in a vast park while up on Holcombe Hill, on the left, stands the memorial to Robert Peel. Again we cross a bend of the river and arrive at Ramsbottom, the present terminus of the line. Beyond the level crossing, on the left is a nineteenth-century church in mock-Romanesque style. Stubbins, a mile farther up the valley, was once the junction with the line to Haslingden and Accrington, long since lifted. Holcombe Moor borders the valley to the west and Scout Moor above Edenfield outlines the horizon to the east. At Alderbottom we cross to the left bank of the river and pass the village of Irwell Vale. After spanning yet another meander of the Irwell the line reaches the station at Ewood Bridge, by the B6527. The end of the line at Rawtenstall is just over a mile away, after burrowing under the M66 and crossing the Irwell one last time. Reopening to here is planned for 1989.

Once a thriving cotton and silk town, Rawtenstall is today known to skiers in the North West for its dry ski slope.

THE RAILWAYS OF THE ISLE OF MAN
by Alan McGiffin

Although only 32 miles long and 10 miles wide, the Isle of Man has some fine and varied scenery, and much to interest the visitor. It is also fortunate to have four narrow-gauge railways and a horse tramway.

Isle Of Man Steam Railway

PORT ERIN — PORT ST MARY — COLBY — BALLABEG — CASTLETOWN — BALLASALLA — SANTON — PORT SODERICK — DOUGLAS

The steam railway station is a large ornate building at the top of the harbour. From April to September some four to five trains daily except Saturdays, run the 15 miles to Port Erin. The 3 foot gauge line is single track with passing loops. Four of the original sixteen tank engines and two railcars are still in use. The passenger carriages are maintained to a high standard, and boast heating and electric lighting. In general the railway is very reminiscent of the Irish narrow-gauge systems at their best.

Leaving Douglas, the line passes its workshops on the right and runs through pleasant countryside to Port Soderick, for the glen and small bay. A standard-gauge tramway ran from here to Douglas until 1939. Santon Halt serves the holiday village and bay at Port Grenaugh. The next station is Ballasalla. The main attractions here are Rushen Abbey Gardens and Silverdale Glen with its old-style pleasure-grounds. There is also a pleasant walk along the Silverburn River to Castletown. Castletown itself is well worth a visit if only for the magnificent Norman castle. The town also has a traditional brewery and a maritime museum. There are some good walks east to Derbyhaven, Langness Point, and Santon Gorge, and west to Scarlett Point and Port St Mary. After Castletown, the line runs through farming country to Ballabeg halt and Colby. The unspoilt and quiet Colby Glen is well worth visiting. Port St Mary offers a good beach and a busy yachting harbour. Good walks are available to Port Erin, Spanish Head and Cregneish Village Museum. Port Erin, the terminus of the line, is a small traditional seaside resort. There are plenty of good hotels and guest-houses to suit every pocket. The sheltered bay provides safe but cold bathing. Boat trips are available to the Calf of Man and there are easy walks to Bradda Head and Fleshwick Bay.

Manx Electric and Groudle Glen Railway

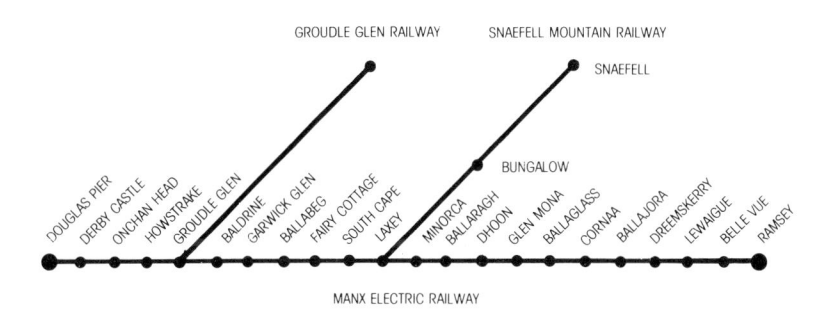

GROUDLE GLEN RAILWAY — SNAEFELL MOUNTAIN RAILWAY — SNAEFELL — BUNGALOW

DOUGLAS PIER — DERBY CASTLE — ONCHAN HEAD — HOWSTRAKE — GROUDLE GLEN — BALDRINE — GARWICK GLEN — BALLABEG — FAIRY COTTAGE — SOUTH CAPE — LAXEY — MINORCA — BALLARAGH — DHOON — GLEN MONA — BALLAGLASS — CORNAA — BALLAJORA — DREEMSKERRY — LEWAIGUE — BELLE VUE — RAMSEY

MANX ELECTRIC RAILWAY

The electric railway station is at Derby Castle near the north end of the Promenade. It can be reached by the Douglas horse trams or Promenade buses. The double-track Douglas–Laxey–Ramsey line is rather like an old-style American inter-urban with d.c. current collection by trolley from an overhead line. A frequent summer service

65

The Laxey Wheel, Isle of Man (*Photo:* Mike Crowhurst)

and limited winter service is operated by single-unit power cars. Open trailers are added in summer.

From Douglas, the line runs as a roadside tramway, following the coast road through Onchan Head and Groudle to Laxey. There are some fine views of Douglas Bay from this section. Groudle is the station for the Glen and holiday village and also a short 2-foot-gauge line which has been restored to a high standard by a dedicated group of volunteers. Laxey is famous for its enormous water-wheel. The quaint harbour and pretty Glen Gardens are also worth a visit. Traditional weaving can be seen at the woollen-mills. The Swiss Chalet-style terminus is shared with the Snaefell Mountain Railway. The line takes a horseshoe route round Laxey Bay, passing the strangely named Minorca halt *en route*. The railway then follows a coastal route with some breath-taking scenery for the next few miles. The fine wooded glens at Ballaglass and Dhoon should not be missed. The unusual beach at Port Cornea is a good walk from Ballaglass. From Ballaglass, the line runs inland to Ramsey. Maughold village and lighthouse can be seen to the east. On the approach to Ramsey, there are panoramic views of the bay and coastline to the north. Ramsey is a pleasant open town with a long promenade and pier. The Mooragh Park Gardens and Rural Life Museum are worth a visit. There is also a small Electric Railway Museum at the station which complements the Steam Museum at Port Erin.

Snaefell Mountain Railway

This is a unique, double track, 3 foot 6 inch gauge system with Fell guide rail and current collection by bow collector from overhead lines. Right-hand running is the rule. Powerful, well-maintained single railcars provide the summer-only service.

The line diverges from the Manx Electric Railway just after the road crossing and climbs steadily up Laxey Glen giving some fine views of the water-wheel and village. The TT course (Ramsey–Douglas mountain road) is crossed at the Bungalow Station. Alight here for the interesting Murray's Motorbike Museum. From the Bungalow the line spirals round to the summit (2,034 feet) where there is a restaurant and some of the best views in the British Isles. On a clear day the whole Isle, and Ireland, Scotland, Wales and England can be seen.

Bus Services
The Douglas–Peel via St John's and the St John's–Ramsey steam lines closed in 1968 and the Foxdale branch in 1948. These routes can still be followed by bus. Peel, famous for its castle and cathedral, can be reached by a good service from Douglas and an infrequent service but a scenic one from Port Erin via Foxdale. St John's is the stop for Tynwald Hill and the craft centre. A route to Ramsey from Douglas runs via the beautiful Glen Helen and the wildlife park at Ballaugh. Other beauty-spots accessible by bus are Niarbyl Bay and the Sound. The various rail/bus Rover tickets are a good investment.

THE LAKESIDE & HAVERTHWAITE RAILWAY
by Tim Young

The line was originally opened from Plumpton Junction near Ulverston to Lakeside with great ceremony on 1 June 1869. Its main scource of revenue in those days was freight—coal for the Windermere steamers, iron-ore for Backbarrow ironworks and sulphur and saltpetre for Black Beck and Low Wood gunpowder works. In the other direction it was pig-iron, gunpowder, pit-props, ultramarine and wooden bobbins from the Finsthwaite area. By the turn of the century, the iron-ore industry had declined but with more modern vessels plying up and down Lake Windermere, the Furness Railway, who owned the line, were in an ideal position to encourage and carry trainloads of day trippers and holiday-makers. During those golden years, the line's future hit a peak just before the First World War, tailing off slightly as cars became more and more popular. On 5 September 1965, British Rail closed the line although it carried freight for a further two years. A brake-van enthusiasts' special was the last train to visit Lakeside on 2 September 1967. It was not reopened until 2 May 1973 under the auspices of the Lakeside & Haverthwaite Railway Company Ltd, and even then only the 3½ miles of line at the north end of the branch was in operation. The late Eric Treacy, then Bishop of Wakefield, performed the opening ceremony.

As one leaves Haverthwaite Station, the train heads on to the crossover to take the left-hand side for Lakeside. The adjacent line up the yard goes to Backbarrow Ironworks. With a high rock face on one's left, we plunge into the darkness of the 87-yards-long East Tunnel. After we emerge into daylight again, the uphill gradient we have been climbing ever since we left Haverthwaite slackens to 1 in 120 as we encounter a sharp left-hand curve. We pass the ruins of the ironworks before enjoying a view over the Leven Valley, the river and waterfall below and the former ultramarine works beyond, recently converted to the Lakeland village, Whitewater Hotel, Timeshare and Leisure Complex. Now a mile from Haverthwaite we climb up a short straight stretch before going round a long right-hand curve passing under a bridge at Linstey Green. Gummers How Peak can be seen in the distance. We pass over the Finsthwaite Road at Cuckoo Bridge and for the next ¾ mile pass forests on one side with sheep and beef-cattle pastures on the other. After this long straight stretch, we

A train leaves Newby Bridge for Haverthwaite on 22 July 1973 (*Photo:* Tom Heavyside)

enter a deep rock cutting, and go under two limestone bridges. The view opens out to reveal a waterfall below an old converted water mill across the fields before we enter Newby Bridge Station. We then go under the Lakeside to Hawkshead road and descend through a cutting to the rear of the Swan Hotel then on to the shore of Windermere itself, passing the handsome cast-iron Landing How Bridge, the Windermere Iron Steamboat company's slipway and winch-house where the steamers are hauled from the water for the winter and for maintenance. Finally we come to the large signal-box at the end of the platform at Lakeside Station. The boat is moored alongside to take us up the lake to Bowness and Ambleside.

The author would like to express his sincere thanks to the Lakeside & Haverthwaite Railway Company Ltd without whose assistance and co-operation this article could not have been written.

THE RAVENGLASS & ESKDALE RAILWAY
by Douglas Ferreira

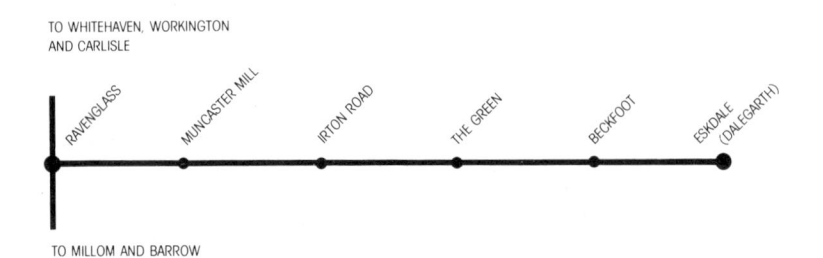

The Ravenglass & Eskdale Railway was first opened to passengers in 1876. The fact that it is still open to them today is a story as colourful and moving as the times it has lived through.

Today, as people from all over the world make the 7-mile journey up the lovely river valleys of the Mite and Esk, those past hundred-odd years may seem very far away. Today, when people join the train at Ravenglass and travel to Dalegarth ready to explore the beautiful countryside round Eskdale, when walks, waterfalls, and rambles are the order of the day, it is easy to forget that 't'laal Ratty', as the line is known, was made for work as well. Just like its well-known narrow-gauge counterparts in Wales, the R & ER was built to link the mines in the fells with transport on the coast. The Eskdale Valley was not so much a beauty-spot then, it was a centre of iron-ore and this had to be transported to the Furness Railway main line at Ravenglass. Within a short time of the line being opened for this purpose, the price of iron-ore dropped dramatically and it was hardly a worthwhile proposition transporting it from Eskdale. The threat to Ratty loomed large for many years. The line operated in Chancery for a long time with the total annual revenue from passenger and goods traffic rarely reaching more than £1,000. Expenses could not be covered, the track became increasingly dangerous, the locomotives were worn out, and the coaches fell into disrepair. For Ratty to survive till 1913 amazed many people, many others objected strongly though when the line was closed it seemed a sad ending for such a short-lived railway. Fortunately, the well-known model making firm of Bassett-Lowke of Northampton had other ideas and acquired the line almost immediately. The 3-foot-gauge track was rebuilt to the new miniature of 15 inches and this brought a new lease of life. One tiny engine appeared, then even bigger and better ones came into service hauling passengers and freight into Eskdale. Although the service was a little erratic at first, it was much appreciated throughout the community.

Ratty lived again carrying mail, provisions and coal into the dale and timber, farm produce, potatoes and hugh sacks of wool away to the market.

It was on this traffic and, later, granite from the quarries that opened up that the railway flourished up until 1953. Once again, just as had happened forty years before with the iron-ore mines, the closure of the granite quarries almost brought the closure of the railway. Even with the tourist traffic, 1959 found Ratty losing money at a constant rate. There was a record season the year it was put up for sale – a mark of the affection in which the railway was held. At the auction of the rolling-stock and properties in 1960, there was a surprising reprieve once again. A band of enthusiasts outbid the scrap-dealers to ensure that 't'laal Ratty' rolled on.

A company was formed to operate the railway and today there is a preservation society of 1,700 members supporting the line. The last twenty-six years have seen the successful refurbishing of track, equipment, locomotives, and rolling-stock with every effort being made to make the whole undertaking self-supporting. Besides new track, locomotives, coaches, and buildings, facilities for the visitors who are all so vital to the line's continued success are always undergoing improvement. In 1974, the company even opened its own pub, The Ratty Arms, a conversion of the old BR station building at Ravenglass.

Although 1975 was the centenary of the opening of the line to goods traffic, most of the centenary celebrations took place in 1976, 100 years from the date when passengers were first carried officially. Unintentionally though very appropriately, the largest steam-engine built in Britain at the time of the celebrations was the one produced in the railway's own workshops at Ravenglass.

Today 100,000 people a year come by car, coach or train to enjoy the unspoilt nature of Eskdale and take a ride on the little railway that is now known all over the world. For all its size, two-thirds of the passengers on 't'Ratty' are adults which suggests that the number of steam-train enthusiasts is far from small and the future of the lines like the Ravenglass & Eskdale are safe from the misfortunes of the past and can look forward to a successful future preserving a great tradition.

THE YORKSHIRE DALES RAILWAY
by John Keavey

Skipton – a historic market town – whose claim to be 'The Gateway to the Yorkshire Dales' is matched by its age-old importance as a sheeptown, used to be an important junction station on the old Midland Railway system, and later, in the days of the LMSR. In pre-Beeching days four lines converged on the town – with a fifth joining it a couple of miles out. Trains ran into Skipton from the Aire Valley (Leeds & Bradford), from Ilkley, with the Grassington branch, Colne from Lancashire, Lancaster & Carnforth from the west, and of course from Settle Junction the famous Settle – Carlisle.

Today Skipton is no longer a junction, at least not for passenger trains, for tickets are only issued for the Aire Valley and stations beyond, and west towards Lancaster and Carlisle. A single freight-only branch runs up to Swinden Quarry on what was once the original Yorkshire Dales Railway to Grassington and Threshfield.

Skipton does have one other ace up its sleeve however, for about 1¼ miles from Skipton Castle there lies an enclave of private enterprise, dubbed recently as a stubborn resurgence – the steam-operated and all-volunteer Yorkshire Dales Railway, known also as 'The Friendly Line'. The YDR operate a 2-mile stretch of line on what was once the Skipton – Ilkley line between Embsay Junction and Holywell halt, with the principal station at Embsay, a short way up the line from Embsay Junction.

The Skipton – Ilkley line closed in 1965, with the Embsay Junction to Embsay stub remaining for residual traffic from the local quarry – but by 1968 this traffic had dwindled to nothing. About this time it seemed likely that the Grassington branch would close too, and a group of local enthusiasts formed the Embsay & Grassington Railway Preservation Society to try and save the line and operate a service of steam trains, using Embsay as a base. 'Twas not to be... Tilcon Ltd took over the Swinden Quarry and launched an expansion programme which included a commitment to rail haulage – so the Swinden section of the branch was refurbished and now carries stone traffic in trainloads. Out of this development was born the Yorkshire Dales Railway Museum Trust and the revised objective of relaying tracks eastwards from Embsay to Bolton Abbey.

There's many a slip and lots of hard work and patience required in rebuilding a railway – but in 1979 the YDR got approval to operate steam trains over the ½ mile of track between Embsay Junction and Embsay. In 1982 the line was extended a further mile to Skibeden loop and as we go to press a further ½ mile is opening to Holywell Halt. The latter is a particularly exciting development because alongside the station a parcel of derelict land has been converted by the MSC into an attractive picnic area and nature trail, complete with running stream. An ideal place on a summer day to get out of the train and stretch the legs. Also at this point the railway cutting has been designated an Area of Special Scientific Interest – with a public viewing platform to inspect an unusual rock formation. Close by Holywell Halt a footpath leads up to the attractive stone-built village of Halton East from which a green road leads up to the heights of Halton Moor – while for those who prefer to explore from Embsay the railway publish guides to a couple of useful footpath trails. There is also a Lead Mining Interpretation Centre at the station. There is a local bus service to Embsay from Skipton, though to walk is quite pleasant, while cyclists will soon cover the distance between town and village.

Future plans envisage the YDR extending through Draughton Bottom and as close as land availability permits to Bolton Abbey.

For the 1987 visitor, YDR offers unlimited rides on its trains on the day of issue of the passenger's ticket. A fully licensed buffet car operates on most trains and the trains are all corridor and smartly turned out. The locomotives, industrial tank engines, the sort one would have seen in quarries, collieries, steelworks, etc. are all brightly liveried and smartly turned out, and in turns cheeky and pugnacious. There is a smart station buffet, a super book and model railway shop, described as 'The best in preservation' — and on selected dates 'Wine and Dine' trains and combined "Murder Mystery and Suspense" bus and train tours. Make haste to The Friendly Line.

Trains operate basically every Sunday from Easter to October, with Saturday and Tuesday trains during July and August — plus Bank Holidays, of course. Special services run around Bonfire Night and during December for Santa Claus trains.

What can the discerning traveller see from the YDR carriage windows? Well, starting from Embsay Junction the view to the left (facing Embsay and Skibeden) is dominated by hills. First there is the heights of Crookrise, followed by the striking mass of Embsay Crag. As the train starts off from the Embsay Junction running round the loop one can see the Grassington branch, or what's left of it, curving round to commence the descent to Skipton. Also on the left as the train climbs the bank up to Embsay (about 1 in 125) the traveller looks out across the lower part of the village — largely modern suburbia, with the older village farther up the hill. To the right there are grassy slopes which soon give way to the old engine house and then the rock-strewn mass of Skipton Rock, Haw Bank, and Skibeden Quarries.

The train will go through Embsay Station at a sedate 10 mph — by order of the Railway Inspectorate — then as the coaches pass the yard and sidings (locomotives shed to the left, carriage sidings to the right) the driver will open up a bit for the steady climb up to Skibeden, just short of the summit of the line. The view to the right is dominated by the quarry and the tree and grass reclamation planting now proceeding, whereas on the left the hills continue to dominate the scene with the road to Barden Tower and Wharfedale climbing up to Black Park and the skyline. A rural lane — which would very probably have been closed years ago for lack of traffic if it had been a railway — parallels the line and after the customary halt at the Skibeden loop the train traverses the summit of the line, drops into a shallow cutting under a footbridge and runs cautiously down grade until the brakes go on for Holywell and our second station.

THE FYLDE COAST – A BRIEF GUIDE
by Tim Young

The Fylde coast stretches from Lytham in the south through to Fleetwood in the north, passing through St Annes, Blackpool, and Thornton Cleveleys *en route*.

Lytham St Annes, comprising Lytham, Ansdell and St Annes-on-the-Sea faces on to the Ribble Estuary. Lytham has no beach but it does have a very attractive area of greensward on which is situated Lytham windmill. Also on the front separated from the sea by the road which runs along the front, is Lowther Gardens with putting, tennis, bowls, etc. Moving along the coast towards Fleetwood, one comes to Ansdell with its large Fairhaven Lake on the front. Not far inland is the Royal Lytham and St Annes golf-course where the 1988 Open Championship will be held. Further round still, we come to St Annes-on-the-Sea. One of its more unusual claims to fame is that the main headquarters of one of the main sporting bodies in this country, the Football League, are to be found here. Its offices can be reached by heading towards the front from the station, and, when you get to the main crossroads, turning left along Clifton Drive. St Annes has a nice beach and a small pier. Unfortunately at low tide the sea is some distance away. However these three resorts are far less commercialised than their neighbouring big brother Blackpool while still having plenty to keep most folk of all ages amused.

There is not much that could be written about Blackpool that has not already been written. Time and space does not permit a full description of everything that one could do on a visit to this, the main resort on the Fylde. It is suggested that you visit the main Tourist Information Centre in a side street behind the Tower, which is the one attraction you cannot miss seeing, and they will be able to help you find the sort of things you like doing on a day at the coast. Blackpool has three piers, two major swimming-pools on the front, the one at the south only having been opened during 1986, and called 'The Sandcastle', designed to look like a tropical lagoon inside. One pays a flat admission charge which then entitles the holder to stay there all day. There are restaurants and other amusements as well as the pools. The Derby Baths, about ½ mile north of the Tower, is somewhat older and is simply a swimming-pool and sauna centre. Inland you will find Stanley Park. This park, almost as large if not larger than some of the major parks everyone knows of in Central London contains a large number of facilities including the famous Blackpool Zoo. In conclusion, Blackpool is highly commercialised, brash and garish. In its favour, though, the writer has never found it a rip-off. True you can spend a fortune especially if you have a family, but most attractions except, possibly, the Tower are modestly priced.

Finally, we come to the twin resorts of Thornton Cleveleys and Fleetwood. Both can be reached by the Blackpool tram, Thornton Cleveleys being the one we come to first, being roughly equidistant between Blackpool and Fleetwood. Like Lytham St Annes it is not devoid of amenities by any stretch of the imagination yet is not as heavily commercialised as Blackpool. One stretch of its beach is prohibited to our canine friends and is cleaned daily into the bargain. Fleetwood, a few miles farther north still, celebrated its 150th anniversary in 1986. As well as being a resort, Fleetwood has also been a port from which one could take a ferry to the Isle of Man. However at the time of writing it is uncertain whether these ferries will continue to sail from Fleetwood in future summers or whether Heysham which now operates the only year-round ferry service to the Isle of Man will maintain its monopoly during the summer, too. Fleetwood has a popular pier and a maritime museum which has a variety of interesting exhibits highlighting its main industry, fishing. Market days in Fleetwood are on Monday, Tuesday, Friday and Saturday during the season. Fleetwood also stands at the mouth of the River Wyre, and a ferry operates to the village opposite which is called Knott End, from which you can take a quiet country or riverside walk.

LANCASTER, MORECAMBE AND HEYSHAM
by Tim Young

The first visible remains of human occupation in Lancaster date from Roman times, although Neolithic settlements can also be traced. Its prosperity came in the eighteenth century, trading with the West Indies. The Customs House was designed by Richard Gillow, son of Robert who in 1764, founded the firm of furniture-makers. Lancaster Castle was built about 1400 by Henry IV, John of Gaunt's son, and has been held by the Crown ever since. Its dramatic gatehouse towers above you. The castle is used as a prison for about 200 men and also houses the Crown Court. You can still have a guided tour each day from Easter until the end of September for a moderate charge, of a financial not criminal nature. Nearby is the Priory Church, outside which you can enjoy spectacular views of the city, its buildings and the imposing green dome of the Ashton Memorial on the hilltop opposite. Other buildings of interest in Lancaster include the Judge's Lodgings, a gracious town house of the seventeenth century which houses the Gillow and Town House Museum as well as a Museum of Childhood. The Town Hall, another legacy of Lord Ashton, is equally as imposing as the more prominent memorial already mentioned. Farther out of the city is Hornsea Pottery, which offers a comprehensive range of facilities for the tourist from Easter to October, including factory tours, gift shops, etc. Lancaster University, about 2 miles south of the city was founded in 1964.

Morecambe, situated on the coast about 4 miles west of Lancaster, is renowned for its bay. At low tide it is possible to walk across the sands to Grange-over-Sands, but it is imperative that you should only do so with one of the local official guides. There are notorious areas of quicksand, and the tide comes in with spectacular speed. In 1985, during a fleeting visit to the North West, His Royal Highness the Duke of Edinburgh drove a coach and four across the bay, under the supervision of one of these guides. Morecambe, however, is a a major resort in its own right. Near the station is Morecambe Leisure Park with a variety of rides and amusements. Its most notable feature used to be a 'Big Wheel' that could be seen for several miles around. However at the end of the 1982 season, it was sold to somewhere in America. Opposite the Leisure Park and station is Marineland, which hosts regular dolphin shows throughout the summer.

Heysham, to the south of Morecambe, is a quaint village that you will love exploring. It is also a port, from which most sailings to the Isle of Man leave the mainland. St Peter's Church in Heysham is over a thousand years old and is also worth a visit.

A few miles to the north is Carnforth whose most well-known attraction is Steamtown, a privately run museum in the old depot and sidings and among whose most renowned exhibits are included *Sir Nigel Gresley* and *Flying Scotsman*. There are steam rides and other exhibits all of which are covered by the basic admission charge. Farther north at Silverdale is Leighton Moss Nature Reserve while nearby is Leighton Hall, family home of the Gillow family, mentioned earlier. There are guided tours and the examples of early Gillow furniture are worthy of note. The other attraction Leighton Hall has to offer is a remarkable display by eagles, hawks, and falcons. Inland from the coast are two Areas of Outstanding Natural Beauty. Beacon Fell Country Park is set in 300 acres of rolling countryside, and Beacon Fell itself offers superb views over most of present-day Lancashire to anyone energetic enough to climb to its summit. Together with the beautiful Trough of Bowland and spectacular underground caves at Ingleton, Beacon Fell Country Park is only accessible to cyclists of a reasonable calibre.

These are but a few of the attractions and amenities, that this particular corner of Lancashire has to offer. There is something for all ages and all tastes and only a thorough exploration of the area will reveal what it has to offer *you*!

LIVERPOOL
by Andrew Macfarlane

Liverpool's name betrays its Welsh origins coming from "Lle'rpwll", the 'place of the pool'. From its beginnings as a fishing village Liverpool grew into the most important port in the North of England and one of its largest cities. The city gained its first Royal Charter in 1207 from King John who needed a new port to replace Chester whose link with the sea, the River Dee, was silting up. The first modern deep-water docks in the world were opened in 1715. In the eighteenth century Liverpool grew prosperous from the slave trade and in the nineteenth century cotton for the mills of Lancashire became its most important source of income. The nineteenth century also saw an influx of immigrants from both Asia and Europe which made Liverpool a multi-national city. Today the city is in relative decline but it can still offer much of interest to the visitor.

Three large buildings dominate the Pier Head – the nearest station is James Street – and help make up one of the most famous waterfronts in the world. The Royal Liver Building, built in 1910, is the most well known. Its twin towers are topped by the legendary Liver Birds. The Cunard Building of 1916 is now the Customs House and the Dock Board Building, headquarters of the Mersey Docks & Harbour Company, dates from 1907. The nearby Church of St Nicholas is worthy of note. The Mersey Maritime Museum is situated round the two Canning Graving Docks and the Canning Half Tide Basin next to the Pier Head. Many of the original dock fittings remain, including cast-iron bollards, capstans, and gate winches. The Boat Hall contains restored full-sized local craft and there are demonatrations of sail- and net-making. A steam-crane and steam-lorry are also on display. There are splendid views across the Mersey to Birkenhead and over to the restored Albert Dock Warehouses, Britain's largest Grade 1 Listed Building, which date from 1845. The five-storey warehouses enabled goods to be transferred directly from ship to storeroom, thus eliminating damage and pilferage.

The foundation-stone of Liverpool's Anglican Cathedral was laid in 1904 but it was not finally completed until 1978. The Gothic design was the work of Sir Giles Gilbert Scott, who was also responsible for London's St Pancras Station and who was, incidentally, a Roman Catholic! The tower is 331 feet high and the cathedral boasts the largest organ in the world, incorporating 10,000 stops. The Metropolitan Cathedral of Christ the King, the Roman Catholic Cathedral, was designed by Sir Frederick Gibberd (who was a Protestant!) and was begun in 1962, being consecrated in 1967. Its circular design enables 2,700 people to worship no farther than 80 feet from the Sanctuary steps. The St George's Hall, a venue for concerts, is a fine example of modern Classical-style architecture with its 60-foot-high Corinthian columns. The Walker Art Gallery and Liverpool City Museum in William Brown Street adjacent to Lime Street Station are both worth a visit. Exhibits in the art gallery include the famous *And when did you last see your father?*, while the City Museum has galleries dealing with prehistoric life, local history and the arts as well as having its own aquarium.

MANCHESTER
by Andrew Macfarlane

If the average tourist were to draw up a list of places in England they would wish to visit Manchester would probably not figure highly, if at all. It does, however, have a great deal to offer those who take the time to seek out its places of interest. Manchester's importance goes back to Roman times when, as Mancunium, it was the junction of seven Roman roads. Agricola's fort has recently been reconstructed and is just one of the attractions of the Castlefield Heritage Park close to Deansgate Station which also contains the Manchester Air and Space Museum and the Greater Manchester Museum of Science and Industry, the latter housed in the former Liverpool Road Station, the original terminus of the Liverpool & Manchester Railway. Cheetham's Hospital School near to Victoria Station is one of the best-preserved examples of a medieval manor and dates from before 1420. It is now one of the top junior music schools in Britain as well as boasting the oldest public library in England which contains some 65,000 books including many valuable and rare volumes. Manchester's Gothic cathedral nearby was built in the Middle Ages and the misericords (tip-up seats) of the choir-stalls which date from 1508 have beautiful carvings illustrating medieval stories and legends. Another interesting building is the half-timbered old Wellington Inn and Sinclair's Oyster Bar behind Marks & Spencer which survived a redevelopment scheme and now rest on concrete stilts. Also worthy of note is the elegant St Ann's Church which is of seventeenth century origin.

Manchester was in the forefront of the Industrial Revolution and its first cotton-spinning mill was opened by Richard Arkwright in 1790. Cotton was the principal reason for the rapid growth of Manchester, which became a city in 1853. The splendid Gothic Town Hall in Albert Square was designed by Alfred Waterhouse and opened in 1877. It was constructed of brick cased in sandstone and its clock tower reaches a height of 281½ feet. The large hall on the first floor has a magnificent panelled ceiling bearing the arms of those towns and countries having business connections with the city as well as those of the Royal Family and the Duchy of Lancaster. The nearby Manchester Central Library with its Classical dome dates from 1934 and is the largest municipal library in England. The 35½-mile-long Manchester Ship Canal links the city with the sea. It took six years to build and was opened by Queen Victoria in 1894. It is 120 feet wide at the bottom and has a minimum depth of 28 feet. Its future, however, is in doubt.

The Manchester Museum in Oxford Road has a very large collection of Egyptian antiquities including several mummies and a furnished funeral chamber. It also houses a collection of ancient rocks and fossils including a fossil forest of the Carboniferous period. The Holy Name Church on the opposite side of Oxford Road

G-Mex (*Photo:* Andrew Macfarlane)

is a fine French Gothic building of 1869 while the John Rylands Library on Deansgate is one of the best examples of Neo-Gothic architecture in Europe, dating from 1900. Finally, visitors to Manchester should not miss the new Greater Manchester Exhibition Centre (or G-Mex for short), the renovated Manchester Central Station dating from 1880. The former train shed, of a similar design to that of London St Pancras, has a span of 210 feet and has been superbly restored after years of neglect.

Attractions outside the city centre include the Greater Manchester Museum of Transport in Boyle Street, Cheetham containing many restored buses in a kaleidoscope of liveries which is open on Saturdays, Sundays, Wednesdays, and Bank Holidays from April to October and the preserved tramway in Heaton Park which carries fare-paying passengers in the summer months.

PRESTON
by Richard Watts

Preston Station is not the most auspicious introduction to the town. The station still lives in the nineteenth century and is cold, unwelcoming, and awkward if you have a suitcase. However, there are ambitious plans to improve this sad state of affairs but progress has been slow. You may well trip over some workmen while leaving the station!

Preston is the main administrative centre for Lancashire and to the north of the station, on the left, is County Hall. This large building was begun in 1878 and incorporates a church.

If you exit right after passing through the ticket barrier you come to the new Fishergate Centre. This is Preston's contribution to the twenty-first century. It is a vast building largely occupying the old goods yard and housing two larger stores and several smaller shops. Of novelty value are the glass lifts – good for taking the children to see!

The Fishergate Centre is at one end of Fishergate, Preston's main shopping street. Walk a short way up this until you come to Chapel Street, where a right turn will take you to Winckley Square. Here are Georgian and Victorian houses built round a very attractive green open space. Continuing down Winckley Square will bring you to Avenham and Miller parks. These two parks together with Winckley Square bring pleasant green parkland right to the heart of the town – Prestonians are justly proud of this.

For the real ale enthusiast a brisk walk through the parks will bring you to The Continental which is situated by the bridge carrying the West Coast main line over the Ribble.

Returning to Fishergate and continuing up the road notice the Miller Arcade on your left, a mock Gothic shopping centre. Turning left by it, and you come to the old Flag Market, which has the Harris Library and Museum, Town Hall, Post Office, War Memorial, and Obelisk round it. Near by is the Guild Hall, this is a very fine entertainment centre and many concerts, plays, and sporting events are held here.

By walking across the Flag Market you will arrive at the 'covered' market. Preston market is open every day and contains indoor and outdoor sections. The outdoor section is held under a very impressive iron roof.

Leading off from the Flag Market is Friargate, Preston's other main shopping street. A short way down Friargate is an entrance to St George's Shopping Precinct. This is a triple-deck shopping centre with a central rotunda and a multi-storey car park above it. Walking through this we come to Lune Street. Turn left, back on to Fishergate, and a few minutes' walk brings you back to the station.

SOUTHPORT
by Tim Young

Southport, a resort full of Victorian charm, is situated at the northernmost tip of the Metropolitan County of Merseyside. Its main shopping street, Lord Street, epitomises the elegance and sophistication that Victorians loved, in the architecture of its shops and department stores, and the gracious style of its arcades.

Between the shops and the sea, are the two large areas of parkland, Victoria Park, which is the venue for Southport's Annual Flower Show, and Princes Park, with its equally large marine lake, and many other facilities including the Southport Theatre and Floral Hall, Southport Zoo, bowling- and putting-greens, and several amusement parks. On the front itself, Southport has a pier, and a full programme of night-life during the season and out of it, as well as fine beaches for the more active.

The 'sporty' set are not forgotten either. Southport and its immediate environs boast no less than six golf-courses, while Southport Cricket Ground hosts at least one fixture each season for Lancashire Cricket Club. The other attraction that is likely to be of interest to readers of this book is Steamport Southport, a centre for preserved steam locomotives and vintage road vehicles situated a few hundred yards off Lord Street near to Southport Railway Station. For those interested in railway history, a visit to the Ribble Bus Station on Lord Street would be worth while as it used to be the northern terminus of a circuitous former route to Liverpool by rail closed in 1952.

Southport is also a good centre for touring—Liverpool is close and easy to visit, as are Wigan, Manchester and Preston.

FURTHER INFORMATION

Tourist Boards

Cumbria Tourist Board,
Ashleigh,
Holly Road,
Windermere,
Cumbria,
LA23 2AQ.
Tel. (09662) 4444.

North West Tourist Board,
The Last Drop Village,
Bromley Cross
Bolton
Lancs,
BL7 9PZ
Tel. (0204) 591511.

Rail Information

Barrow 0229 20805
Blackburn 0254 662537/8
Blackpool 0772 59239
Carlisle 0228 44711
Crewe 0270 255245
Lancaster 0524 32333

Liverpool 051 709 9696
Manchester 061 832 8353
Preston 0772 59439
Southport 0704 31727
Warrington 0925 32245
Wigan 0942 42231

Steam Operators

The Lakeside & Haverthwaite Railway Company Ltd, Haverthwaite Station, Ulverston, Cumbria, LA12 8AL. Tel. (0448) 31594.

The Ravenglass & Eskdale Railway Company Ltd, Ravenglass, Cumbria, CA18 1SW. Tel. (06577) 226.

The Yorkshire Dales Railway, Embsay Station, Skipton, North Yorkshire, BD23 6AX. Tel. (0756) 4727.

Isle Of Man Railways, Terminus Building, Strathallan Crescent, Douglas, Isle of Man. Tel. (0624) 4646.

Manx Electric Railway, Derby Castle Station, Douglas, Isle of Man. Tel. (0624) 4549.

The East Lancashire Railway, Bury Bolton Street Station, Castlecroft Road, Bury, Lancs. Tel. 061 764 7790.

Bus Information

Crosville Motor Services Ltd, Crane Wharf, Chester, CH1 4SQ. Tel. (0244) 315400.

Greater Manchester PTE, PO Box 429, County Hall, Piccadilly Gardens, Manchester, M60 1HX. Tel. 061 228-7811.

Blackburn Borough Transport, 15–17 Railway Road, Blackburn, Lancs, BB1 5AZ. Tel (0254) 51112.

Burnley & Pendle Joint Transport Committee, Queensgate, Colne Road, Burnley, Lancs, BB10 1HH. Tel. (0282) 25244/5.

Hyndburn Borough Transport, 142 Blackburn Road, Accrington, Lancs, BB5 1RD. Tel. (0254) 33657.

Preston Borough Transport, Central Bus Station, Preston, Lancs,, PR1 1YX. Tel. (0772) 53671.

Warrington Borough Transport, Wilderspool Causeway, Warrington, Cheshire, WA4 6PT. Tel. (0925) 34296.

Ribble Motor Services Ltd, Frenchwood Avenue, Preston, PR1 4LU. Tel. (0772) 54754.

Merseyside PTE, 24 Hatton Garden, Liverpool, L3 2AN. Tel. 051 236-7676.

Barrow Borough Transport, Hindpool Road, Barrow-in-Furness, Cumbria, LA14 2PE. Tel. (0229) 21325.

Blackpool Borough Transport, Blundell Street, Blackpool, Lancs, FY1 5DD. Tel. (0253) 23931. (This address and telephone number applies for inquiries regarding Blackpool's trams, too).

Isle Of Man Passenger Transport Board, Terminus Building, Strathallan Crescent, Douglas, Isle of Man. Tel. (0624) 73307/8.

Lancaster City Transport, Heysham Road Bus Depot, Morecambe, Lancs, LA3 1DD. Tel. (0524) 424555.

Rossendale Transport, 8 Bacup Road, Rawtenstall, Rossendale, Lancs, BB4 7ND. Tel. (0706) 217777.

J.Fishwick & Sons, Golden Hill Garage, Golden Hill Lane, Leyland, Nr Preston, Lancs. Tel. (0772) 52430.

Fylde Borough Transport, Squire's Gate, Lytham St Annes, Lancs, FY8 2SH. Tel. (0253) 48247/8.

Cumberland Motor Services Ltd, Tangier Street, Whitehaven, Cumbria. Tel. (0946) 3780/1/2/3/4.

Other Books in the Series

North East by Rail *Midlands by Rail*
Scotland by Rail *Cheshire & North Wales by Rail*
Yorkshire by Rail *Kent & East Sussex by Rail*
Five Shires by Rail (E and N Midlands) *South West by Rail*
East Anglia by Rail

All of the above are obtainable from the RDS Sales Officer, Geoff Kent, 21 Fleetwind Drive, East Hunsbury, Northampton, NN4 0ST, from the respective local branches, from bookshops, or from the publishers, Jarrold Colour Publications, Barrack Street, Norwich NR3 1TR.

COME AND JOIN US!

The Railway Development Society is a national, voluntary, independent body which campaigns for better rail services, for both passengers and freight, and greater use of rail transport.

It publishes books and papers, holds meetings and exhibitions, sometimes runs special trains and generally endeavours to put the case for rail to politicians, civil servants, commerce and industry, and the public at large; as well as feeding users' comments and suggestions to British Rail management and unions.

Membership is open to all who are in general agreement with the aims of the Society and subscriptions are:

Standard rate: **£7.50**
Reduced rate (for pensioners, full-time students): **£4**
Families: **£7.50** plus **£1** for each member of the household
Special rates also apply for corporate bodies.

Write to the Membership Secretary, Mr F.J. Hastilow, 21 Norfolk Road, Sutton Coldfield, West Midlands, B75 6SQ.

The North West branch covers most of the area covered by this book, while the Yorkshire branch covers that part of the book within its county boundary. The secretaries of the two branches are:

Andrew Macfarlane, 16 Willow Green, Knutsford, Cheshire, WA16 6AX. Telephone (0565) 53554.

D.J.Bradbury, 59 Dore Road, Dore, Sheffield, S17 3ND. Telephone (0742) 351037.

Local Rail Users' Groups

Ormskirk–Preston Travellers' Association (OPTA). J. E. Berry, 62 Rivington Drive, Burscough L40 7RP.

Derwent Railway Society. R. K. Demain, Oakgarth, Rickerby Lane, Portinscale, Keswick, Cumbria, CA12 5RH.

Friends of the Settle–Carlisle Line Association (FOSCLA). Peter Lawrence, Scar Garth, Church Street, Giggleswick, Settle, N. Yorks BD24 0BE.

Lakes Line Action Group (LLAG). Malcolm Conway, 6 Summer How, Shap Road, Kendal, Cumbria, LA9 6NY.

South Fylde Line Users' Association (SFLUA). Vernon Smith, 66 Holmefield Road, St Annes.

Support the East Lancashire Line Association (STELLA). M. Course, 40 Hall Street, Colne, Lancs, BB8 0DJ.

Support the Oldham, Rochdale, Manchester Line Group (STORM). Peter Dawson, telephone: 061 678-4617.

INDEX

Aintree 40
Ambleside 23, 68
Angus Castle 53
Appleby 33
Arkholme 21
Ball, Alan 49
Beacon Fell Country Park 73
Beeching, Dr. 10, 18
Besses 'o' the Barn 53
Big Wheel 73
Blackpool Pleasure Beach 16, 62, 63
Blackpool Tower 13, 14, 50, 63
Blea Moor 30, 31
Bold Venture Park 51
Bowker Vale 52, 54
British Commercial Vehicle Museum 50
Burnley Manchester Road 56
Bury Transport Museum 64
Chat Moss 35, 47
Chorley 50
Cleveleys 63, 67, 71, 72
Clitheroe 18, 19, 22
Coniston 27
Co-op Stores 56
Coppernob 27
Coppull 7
Copy Pit 56
Crompton, Samuel 51
Cromwell, Oliver 50
Crow Nest Junction 47, 51
Cuerden Valley Country Park 17
Dalesrail 18, 19, 22
Delph 58
Dent 31, 32
Dibnah, Fred 50
Douglas, I.O.M. 12, 65
Eden Valley 29, 32, 33
Edinburgh, The Duke of 73
Eskdale 67, 68, 69
Everton 40
Fields, Gracie 53, 56
Flag Market 76
Fleetwood 12, 13, 62, 63, 71, 72
Flying Arches 50
Football League 71
Forest of Bowland 19
Furness Railway 27, 28, 67, 68
Garden Festival 46

G-Mex 75, 76
Gooch, Sir Daniel 38
Granada TV 34, 49
Grand National 40
Greater Manchester Museum of Transport 76
Hag Fold 47
Halli'th'Wood 51
Hansom, J. 8, 42
Heaton Park 52, 76
Henry VIII 23, 40
Hest Bank 9, 27
Heysham 9, 20, 27, 72, 73
Hoghton Tower 17, 42
Holker Hall 27
Holme Tunnel 56
Huskisson, William 35
Ingleborough 21, 31
Jaffa Cakes 40
Japanese Pond 53
Juliet Bravo 18
Jumbles Country Park 51
Kendal Mint Cake 23
Keswick 10
Knott End 72
Lakeside 23, 67
Lancashire Witches 42
Last Drop Village 51
Laxey 65, 66
Leighton Hall 29, 73
Leighton Moss 29, 73
Liver Birds 74
Liverpool & Manchester Railway 34, 37
Liverpool Rd. Stn., Manchester 35, 74
Locke, Joseph 8, 10
Long Meg 33
Manxman 12
Marks & Spencer 46
Martin Mere 12
Midge Hall 41, 42
Mill Dam Lane 40
Misericords 75
National & Provincial Building Society 55
Natterjack Toads 39
Nelson 18
Olive Mount Cutting 37

Pacers 14, 17, 40, 44
Pendle Hill 19, 22, 42
Queen, Her Majesty the 6, 47
Rainhill 35, 36
Ravenglass 26, 67, 68, 69
Ribblehead 31
Rivington Pike 50
Rochdale Pioneers 54
Rocket 36
Roses Link 18, 56
Rufford Old Hall 41
St Michaels 46
Salford Crescent 47, 49
Sandcastle 16, 63, 72
Sellafield 26
Silverdale 27, 29, 73
Skem Jazzer 40
Slacks 39
Smith, Cyril 56
Sough Tunnel 51
Sprinters 37
Stalybridge Buffet 61
Starr Gate 62, 63
Steamport Southport 12, 77
Steamtown Carnforth 9, 21, 29, 73
Stephenson, George 35, 36
Stoodley Pike 55
Strangeways 60
Summit Tunnel 56
Tate & Lyle 40, 50
Trough of Bowland 73
Turton Towers 51
Ullswater 10, 33
Vampire Jets 33
Vimto 50
Walburge's Street 8, 12, 42
Waterloo 39
Weaver's Triangle 18
Wellington, Duke of 36
Whalley 19
Wigan Pier 6, 7, 47, 48
Windermere 10, 23, 67
W'mere Iron Steamboat Co. 23, 68
Windsor Link 35, 49
Winter Hill 50, 53
Wordsworth, William 10, 23
Wrea Green 14

ISBN 0-7117-0297-7
© 1987 Railway Development Society
Published and printed in Great Britain by Jarrold and Sons Ltd, Norwich. 187.